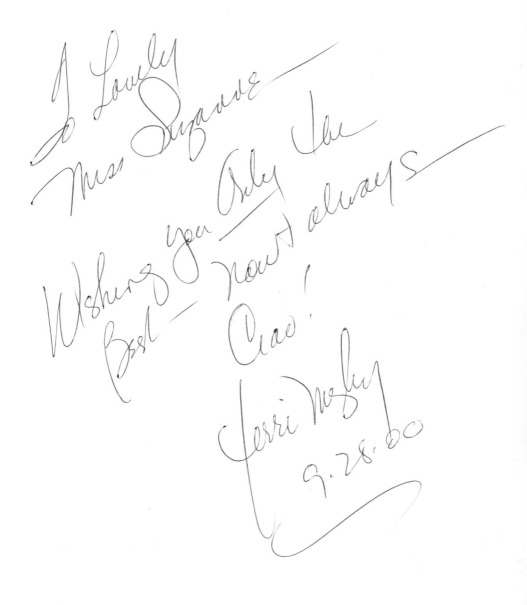

To Lovely
Miss Suzanne —

Wishing you Only the
Best — Now & always

Ciao!

Terri Mobley
9.28.00

TERRI MURPHY'S LISTING & SELLING SECRETS

How To Become A Million $ Producer

Terri Murphy

Real Estate
Education Company
a division of Dearborn Financial Publishing, Inc.

Dedication

To all those new recruits who want to get into real estate because they love houses and people.

Acquisitions Editor: Christine Litavsky
Managing Editor: Jack Kiburz
Interior Design: Lucy Jenkins
Cover Design: Design Alliance, Inc.

© 1996 by Dearborn Financial Publishing, Inc.®

Published by Real Estate Education Company®,
a division of Dearborn Financial Publishing, Inc.®

Printed in the United States of America

98 10 9 8 7 6 5 4 3

Library of Congress Cataloging-in-Publication Data

Murphy, Terri.
  Terri Murphy's listing & selling secrets : how to become a million $ producer / by Terri Murphy.
         p.   cm.
  ISBN 0-7931-1545-0 (cloth)
    1. Real estate listings.   2. Real estate business.   3. Real estate agents
  I. Title.
  HD1382.6.M87   1995
  333.33'068'8—dc20   95-23366
                                                                 CIP

Acknowledgments

As is often the case in life, an outcome rarely is the result of a singular effort. The wonderful individuals who helped create this book will be endeared to my heart forever—from my heart to yours, a most sincere and loving thank you.

To my gifted and generous friend and mentor, Viki King, whose brilliant guidance as an author gave me the vision to write. Hugs to Judith Briles for sharing her time and expertise. My special thanks to Ed DesRoches, who gave me my first opportunity to write that little paragraph in *The Real Estate Professional*—the beginning of more—thank you, Ed, for the gift of opportunity.

Hugs to Paul Seveska, who took the chance to let me write my first weekly column. Thanks to the *Real Estate Today* group, which offered unlimited sources of good information and great guidance. My thanks to Marc and Wendy Jacobson for providing the port in the storm so this work could be completed; to Spiderman, for his fabulous self, genius talent and forever friendship, who challenged me beyond my own expectations; and to Terry Penza, a great resource and most gifted and sharing lady, who always had time to answer questions, especially computer ones!

Eternal thank yous to my staff and those supporters—Pat Lenhoff, Susan Riley, Kathy Goffee, Manny Patterson, the Antos boys and Joan Routledge—for their assistance and big-time patience, and to Samuel A. Libert for nurturing the confidence factor in me to believe it could be done. To Danielle Kennedy, who set a great example of high standards and is a most wonderful role model and mentor. To the great patience of my editor, Christine Litavsky, who is the best example of tough and tender. Love to Og Mandino, whose powerful words from *Mission Success* steeled me through the dark times and to whom I am eternally grateful to have shared time and space.

To Edward S. Peters for providing the lessons of vision, growth and contribution. Forever love to Danny and Theo Cox, whose friendship, caring and mentorship are among my greatest treasures in this lifetime. To Les Brown for sharing his greatness and generosity of spirit.

And to all my super top producers who were generous enough to share with me, especially in the "early" days—Bob Wolff and my best friend and "sister," Stevie D. Clark; Howard Brinton and Barb Burke for the gifts of Star Power; and my Star Power buddies. And a sincere thank you to all those tough customers and clients who provided the challenges that produced the "good stuff" experience is made of.

Contents

Preface

$\mathcal{I}$t seems to me that just about everyone who fancies himself or herself a real estate trainer has something in print, and many of the books on the market today are very good. What do I have to offer?

Well, to answer that question, I have a lot to give back to the industry, and if I had to list the reasons why I would write a book, they would read something like this: First of all, I am currently listing and selling real estate. By that, I mean that I sell residential real estate every day in a competitive market and that my marketplace can be thought of as a representative sampling of most of the United States. I have survived the busy markets and have relished the boom markets. I have been through money shortages, housing shortages and consumer shortages and also have experienced the exact opposite. Simply stated, I have paid my dues and have earned the right to share my experiences with others. Danielle Kennedy, an extraordinary woman and one of my role models as well as one of the world's premier real estate speakers and trainers, once told me that "successful people love to share their experiences. It is a way of giving something back to a society that has provided them the opportunity to succeed." That's reason enough for me. What better way to share my success and ideas than to write a book?

Secondly, I like doing creative things. What can be more creative than becoming an author? I began my adventure in the real estate business with very little confidence and self-esteem. I had little access to seminars and learning and far less support from those within the industry in my market area. I very much want to tell others who are just beginning in the sometimes confusing profession of real estate that many of us "seasoned pros" were just as scared and unsure at the beginning, too. There is so much more now than was available to me. You can make it in today's real estate environment with hard work and dedication, because there are more avenues available for learning. Hopefully, this book will be among your frequent sources of interaction and research.

In any case, I decided to make the commitment and write the book. I sincerely want to share with you some of the growing pains and joys, disappointments and successes that I experienced. I want to open my heart to you as I share with you those things that really helped me learn the ropes.

Please join me in a fascinating exploration of a subject that has been so much a positive part of my life. I welcome your input. If you would like to offer any suggestions or if you want to share your thoughts and ideas, please write me. I'd love to hear from you.

Hugs!

—Terri Murphy, GRI, CRS, LTG

Chapter 1

*L*earning the Secrets of Real Estate

*W*hy should I write a book on real estate? There are plenty of very qualified people who have already done so. The answer is this: I couldn't even drive my car with confidence down a two-lane street in my town, and real estate gave me an outstanding opportunity to discover myself. In the beginning I was afraid of my own shadow, certain that people would know I had no experience and sure that every other person was better at it than me. It just was not true for me, nor for you! I have gathered immense treasures in experience, challenge, victory and self-satisfaction, and magnificent experiences in my travels. And I know by sharing some of these stories with you, maybe I can make your road a little easier and a little more comfortable.

My Own Tale

My first year in the real estate business was just OK. I wasn't a failure, but no one could call me a winner either. I was suffering from the all-too-common malady of allowing everyone and everything to volunteer their "two cents" about my already confused career path. I was a victim of "opinionitis," that state of being where everybody's opinions but my own invaded daily decision making and where others shaped my thoughts to reflect their point of view. I would listen to one opinion and adopt that way of thinking for a while—a day or two at least, or until I was exposed to another opinion. With opinionitis, every opinion is right at the time it is freely given.

In my case, too many conflicting signals were being telegraphed from all sides. The news media were telling me that things were not good in residential real estate, while my broker was saying that plenty of business was available out there and any hardworking agent could find it. On reflection 17 years later, they were both right. Yes, the market was in fairly bad shape but not as bad as it was going to get. If I had known, I probably would have hung my hat on the opinions of those with negative thoughts and retreated to my previous world of fixed paychecks and eight-hour days.

Interest rates were at a record high in 1978, and there was a wait-and-see attitude on the part of the homebuying public. In general, the typical homebuyer was being squeezed out of the market as more than 60 percent of those who were qualified to buy a home a few years earlier could no longer afford one. It was truly a mixed-up market. At the same time, some property owners who had to sell were willing to negotiate in very favorable ways. In fact, the market was not nearly as good as my broker wanted me to think it was, but it was not nearly as bad as prophets of doom were preaching in the news media. Who was I to believe?

*M*urphy's *L*aw

---

*H*ousing is after all a necessity, because sleeping under your car is not an option.

No matter what the interest rates, business climate or zoning laws, people need to own a home. As the real estate agent, you are charged with the duty of selling them, and somehow there always will be a way. Some agents in my own office were convinced that real estate, especially in and around the Chicago area, was a bad deal, yet they were out selling it every day. Opinionitis was rampant!

On top of all this confusion, I was having doubts about fitting into what appeared to be a very nonstructured and freewheeling business. You see, before entering the entrepreneurial state of being a real estate agent, I was living in a very secure world of total organization as an executive secretary to a top-notch builder. In this position, it was my job to keep my immediate boss totally organized, which I did. I organized meetings and coordinated and prepared agendas. Of course, all correspondence was screened and return letters written. My boss just whizzed in and out of the office.

I was living in a very organized world indeed, and it was also a world where I was highly respected. Being a top-notch executive assistant and being privy to many inside secrets, power plays and maneuvers was exciting and very rewarding. I walked with financial and corporate dignity, and I was very proud of my position.

Why on earth leave this world, you ask? Well, the answer was, and still is, simple. I wanted to be in a position to write my own paycheck and earn as much money as I was willing to work for. The business of selling real estate gave me the vehicle I needed to make much more money as an independent businesswoman and, at the same time, required a comparatively small start-up expense. As a real estate agent, I had only to join the local Multiple Listing Service and I was immediately in charge of close to a billion dollars' worth of inventory. My only cash outlay was membership dues, and my first day on the job I had hundreds of homes to show.

But my transformation into a real estate agent was, to say the least, a shock. The world of real estate selling can be disorganized, especially for a first-year agent. My bewilderment was almost constant. The way some of my fellow real estate agents conducted their business lives was totally foreign to me and went against all of the tenets of my previous training. They were late to office meetings, and sometimes they never showed up at all. Their desks were often unrecognizable with "stuff" piled randomly; some of them even took two-hour lunches regularly. In the world of real estate sales, nobody seemed to take orders. They all kept saying that they were independent contractors and that they could do anything they wanted.

The Making of a Salesperson

Here I was, right in the middle of all this so-called independence stuff, all of which conflicted with my incredibly stable background. I did not handle challenges well. I had to get over my fear of even driving a car—a prerequisite in the real estate business, because walking the buyer from house to house would take a lot of time and energy. Things of this independence bent had never come easily to this somewhat sheltered Italian girl raised in a strict old-world, old-fashioned but very loving family. Now, here I was selling real estate! In my neighborhood, Italians never moved. They bought a house and actually paid for it on the installment plan—a 30-year loan. After it was paid for, the normal means of transfer of title was through a will!

I was terrified that someone—a customer, a lender, a fellow real estate agent, my broker or someone else—would find out that I had no experience, even less confidence and absolutely no concept of what it was to move from one house to another more than once in a lifetime.

Besides that, I did not like what I kept hearing about the bad reputations of some people who sold things, especially those high-pressure salespeople. I was determined never to garner such a terrible label. I knew there must be a way to be of service in this industry with an attitude of professionalism. Maybe that's why I worked so hard during my first year in real estate and made so little money. I was afraid to speak to a prospect about anything that would suggest the prospect should place a home on the market or perhaps purchase that nice house down the street.

I was a very good conversationalist—a commercial visitor, so to speak—but not a professional salesperson. I thought that if I actually maneuvered someone into a position to purchase what was really very good for them, I would be using that terrible *high pressure* that all those so-called crooked agents used. "I'm not in the used-car business and I don't sell vacuum cleaners door to door; I'm a professional" was my rationalization. It was, of course, the wrong rationalization, and because of this soft thinking many of my customers were not helped to buy that dream home for themselves and their families.

But there is more. I did seek training, and those who were conducting the seminars kept making suggestions that I should go out and do such things as cold call. That's right, they wanted me to just go out and meet people I had never seen before, on the stranger's turf no less, and who had no idea who I was. Not only that, I was supposed to use some canned speech to get them to say yes to what I wanted. Not only was this time-consuming, I reasoned, but it went against my conception of what I was supposed to do for a living.

Somehow I had managed to rationalize in my real estate dreams that I would just go into my office, sit behind my desk and wait for a qualified customer to call or to walk in. Somehow, maybe through mental self-protection, I never thought for a minute that I would actually have to go out into the town and meet people. But I guess I had selling mixed up with clerking. You know the difference: When a customer surprises the salesperson, that's clerking, but when the salesperson surprises the customer, that's selling.

The Turning Point

I had to sort some things out for myself, and I did. I listened to what others were saying and then compared what was said to how well these people were doing financially and personally, or at least how I perceived their financial and personal well-being. There seemed to be a correlation here. Those real estate agents who looked upon the real estate business positively and treated it as a full-time profession were, for the most part, doing quite well.

The key step was to model myself after those who were at the top of the profession, not just with great listing and selling numbers, but with integrity and a true commitment to service. I only wanted to emulate people who were full-time agents and were involved on the local, state and national level of the industry. It was apparent that I had a true desire to be the best I could be, and using the best as models made good sense.

The second key step in getting up to speed was doing research. I read. I read just about everything that was printed about the real estate business, or so it seemed. I devoured magazine articles and kept abreast of the Sunday real estate sections in my three area newspapers. My most important sources of information regarding real estate trends and professionalism were the National Association of REALTORS® magazine, *Real Estate Today*, and *The Real Estate Professional*. I read a number of "how to sell" real estate books. Some were very good and practical. Most were not. The authors seemed to fall into three categories:

1.   Those who had long and productive careers as real estate salespersons;
2.   Those who had a knack for writing but who were never very successful as real estate practitioners; and
3.   Those who offered a very quick fix to a successful career.

Of the three categories, the quick-fix no-brainers were very popular, and their underlying similarity was to offer a specific set of things to do to set the reader on the "royal road to riches." The one outstanding similarity common to all of these quick-fix approaches to building a long-term career was that hard work and self-discipline were not needed. "Just follow my infallible system and buy my cassette tapes and you will be the envy of your real estate office," was the general theme.

I stuck with the first category of authors, the ones written by those who actually had proven themselves with long and productive careers in the business of selling residential real estate. I decided to pull the best ideas from a cross-section of these books. I used those ideas that seemed to fit my personality, and I kept working on my new skills until I was polished in their use. After a few years I began to understand the secrets of my success and the success of other real estate agents. There is no one set way of successfully listing and selling residential real estate, but some basic similarities of listing and selling techniques are consistent.

I also did my own market research driving through the area and studying the housing. I became an expert on the number of houses in each development, how many of each model were constructed, where on the block different floor plans were built, which had great locations.... I reached the point where I knew the real estate market in my area better than anybody else!

This knowledge was reflected in the way I presented myself to my customers and clients. I carried myself with a new dignity, and when I spoke, my clients just knew that I could help them deal with their own real estate issues. So if real estate is your game, here are some last-minute things to think about as you consider entering this new world.

In the Beginning

You've made the decision to make real estate your career. I'd like to share a checklist with you as a sort of survival kit to getting started, to help you cross the bridge from "brand new" to "look at me now!"

It's all about lasting power. A great rule of thumb is to have ready cash to ease you into the unpredictable world of the real estate paycheck. I won't be the one who says it will take at least a few months to collect dollars; I don't want to limit your thinking. However, the real estate industry has been known to fall prey to a little of Murphy's influence about the best-laid plans. If you are depending on your new career to handle the normal costs of living, like mortgages, groceries and fuel, set yourself up with from three to six months of living money to allow you to concentrate on learning the ropes of your new business.

Find a Mentor

A fantastic way to learn about the business is to begin as a buyer assistant for a busy top producer in your office. The Star Power agent needs people who are committed to learning and doing the best job and want to start with one phase of the business. Being a buyer assistant to a top producer gives you lots of opportunity to develop hands-on experience, while working under the guidance of a seasoned agent. Taking that agent's buyers out to show properties affords you a steady stream of customers without the hassle of generating new business and handling the paperwork. This arrangement will differ with each agent, but there are sales agents who cannot handle all the buyer leads that they receive and are only too happy to turn over the showing part to an enthusiastic "let me at 'em" new person. Compensations vary as well. Some agents offer a percentage, others have bonus arrangements. Ask around and see if this type of a system works for you.

Another alternative for the more conservative individual is the personal assistant program. I have personally trained several people who started out doing the clerical and marketing duties to assist me. There are several successful top producers who will hire you knowing that the position is one of training and will last about one year. After that time, you might consider working as a buyer assistant agent for this top producer and eventually developing your own circle of business. Where there is a will, there is a way.

Let's Do Lunch!

Still a little apprehensive? The best investment you can make is to take a top producer to lunch or dinner. Tell them why you would like to make an appointment and ask if they would be willing to help you reach a decision. The money will be extremely well spent. Don't be afraid to ask all kinds of questions to help you reach a point of confidence and conviction.

- How much did you make the first year?
- How did you handle family obligations?
- Did you provide for your tax obligations?
- What was your formula?
- Did you get special disability insurance?
- When did you hire a part-time assistant?
- How do you pay the people who help you?
- What duties in your home and business did you find necessary to delegate?
- What was your biggest challenge?

These are some of the questions that you will need to answer before making the full commitment to the world of real estate.

Have a Serious Talk with Your Accountant

One of the biggest mistakes a rookie makes is not understanding the new status of being an independent contractor, especially when it comes to our friends the IRS. Those commission checks look pretty healthy compared to the regular corporate paychecks you may have been used to getting. The challenge is to learn how to run your new business like a real business. Things are a little different here in our sales world. It's great to be able to write off several more things than in another type of business; however, this requires very clear and orderly bookkeeping. Here is the key:

If you do it right every day, you won't have the nightmare of re-creating April 15th!

Find an accountant who already works with several real estate agents and who keeps up with the ever-changing requirements of the IRS. Keep excellent track of business mileage, office-related expenses and marketing costs. Learn how to read a profit and loss statement.

Chris Bird, tax expert and part of Howard Brinton's Star Power team, has 16 years' experience as an IRS employee. He offers a wealth of experience and in-depth understanding of tax issues particular to the real estate agent. Not only does he speak the language of the IRS, he offers up-to-the-minute information for the real estate industry. Ask the right questions up-front so you don't get tangled up a year later owing a ton of taxes due to poor planning or just plain ignorance.

Develop a Business Plan

Just showing up and going on caravan as a new agent won't pay the bills or build financial freedom. The industry is in a tremendous transition and requires you to invest both your time and money in a real business that needs vision, direction and purpose as a viable profit center. David D'Arcangelo of San Diego, California, is considered the ultimate financial coach on developing a practical guide to everyday money management. The option of "swinging" without a net is not only risky but also doomed to fail. Make an appointment and pay a top adviser like David to help you form a plan that works for you. This is probably one of the most critical areas for you as a new entrepreneur to understand. Fail to plan, and you plan to fail!

There are four steps to approach the productive listing and selling business. To be successful you need to have a game plan, especially in the beginning. The next chapter describes these four steps that will help you understand the course from rookie to superstar!

Chapter 2

7he Four Steps to a Successful Real Estate Career

7here is always power in knowledge. For the beginner, there is an unmistakable confidence that comes with understanding the products available in the marketplace. Step one requires some due diligence, which means you need to devote some time and energy to getting familiar with the terrain. A better understanding of the industry can be gained with four simple steps.

Step One: Understanding the Marketplace

It is rare, and even theoretical, for any real estate market to exist in total economic balance. (The people with degrees in economics refer to balance as equilibrium.) For such an equilibrium to exist there must be a good number of ready, willing and able buyers chasing a plentiful supply of housing product. If this utopia were to exist, and it sometimes does for short periods, there would be plenty of sales for all, and house prices would never rise above the normal dollar inflation.

*M*urphy's *L*aw

---

*Y*ou don't ever have to worry about a perfect real estate market existing for too long, simply because there are too many forces acting to disrupt our perfect world.

As soon as a lender finds out that too many people are applying for its loans, up goes the interest rate and down goes the number of qualified buyers. Our perfect equilibrium now favors the lending industry and not our buyers and sellers. In some parts of the country, just when a slew of builders are beginning to construct affordable houses, some city council member may decide that it's time for a little moderation of growth. With the advent of one council meeting, a housing shortage is created that forces prices up. The city of Santa Barbara, California, although a very beautiful place, is an example of this kind of economic tinkering.

The facts are very plain: There will never be a perfect real estate market that is all things to all people. Either too many buyers chase too few houses for sale or too many houses for sale chase too few buyers. And because real estate is a credit-intensive industry, if a perfect buyer/seller equilibrium is ever obtained, then some lender will figure a way to change the way a house or a buyer is qualified for a loan. Get the point? I hope so. If you don't, then you are probably selling residential real estate in an area where the economic balance is just right—for now. Don't worry. Just like the weather, the situation will change.

If this market were to exist for long it would eventually be discovered by the unemployed or those wanting to change occupations, and soon there would be too many real estate agents competing for too few sales, and somebody would soon be having trouble paying the bills.

From my point of view, lenders and city zoning commissions only react to what buyers and sellers are creating. It takes three parties to make a good or a bad real estate market:

1. The seller
2. The buyer
3. The real estate salesperson

If the buyer and seller get together without the salesperson, then there would be no point in having a brokerage industry. If too many salespeople come into a good market, it will be harder for the average salesperson to make a living. If too few salespeople work in a terrible market, those who are still selling will make a lot of money. That's why it is very common for some real estate agents to earn a veritable fortune when the press is screaming that the real estate industry is experiencing a depression.

Step Two: Understanding the Challenging Market

In 1989 I gave a talk to the annual Alaska Association of REAL-TORS® Convention in Fairbanks and prepared a program for this group as I always do. First I studied the local and regional residential real estate market conditions; then I put together a presentation that fit the current scene. I was shocked when I found out that most of the state of Alaska was experiencing a true real estate depression—the kind you only read about but never have to experience. Alaska's largest city, Anchorage, was suffering from a population loss, and one out of eight houses was either abandoned or vacant. (Some say it was one out of six houses. I'll go with the optimistic figure.) Fairbanks, 355 miles to the north, was even worse. After further investigation, I found that listing any house in these two cities was out of the question, since the loan balance for the typical home exceeded the current market value of the property. Some homes that had originally sold for $140,000 were bringing prices of less than $80,000, and some duplexes in the town of Wasilla, Alaska, that had commanded a price, when built, of $140,000 were being appraised at $39,500. Houston, Texas, never had it so good!

I went to the convention expecting to see rag-tag, almost welfare-stricken agents and was shocked to meet a terrific group of very successful, solid-as-a-rock real estate professionals. There weren't many of them but they were all making very good money. Why? When the market began collapsing there were, for a short period, too many real estate agents vying for too little business, a typical economic equilibrium out of whack. The standard way of selling real estate through first listing a property for sale and then marketing it through the normal selling techniques simply did not work. Some agents were averaging two listings a day and none of them were selling.

What *was* selling were repossessions, because they were priced at the present deflated market values. Most agents could not see these obstacles as opportunities and did not switch from the conventional listing and selling sales techniques until it was too late. They were too steeped in tradition and inflexible, as is true in many situations where people refuse to learn new things. These agents soon began to look for another line of work. They simply could not recognize the opportunity in the challenge.

The agents that were left, however, found a very good market—in fact, a terrific market. That is, if they had the foresight to change their selling techniques to fit a repossession marketplace. Newcomers who wanted to own their own homes were still moving to Alaska. It didn't make economic sense for them to take over high-interest, inflated loans, but buying a low-down-payment, low-interest repossession did make sense.

I guess no one told Bob Wolff when he owned the Fort Collins, Colorado, residential listing and selling market that business was supposed to be bad. Bob continued to sell $12–$15 million of real estate each year despite the fact that Colorado was experiencing its worst real estate market since the Great Depression.

An event as traumatic as an earthquake did not keep Debra Berman and Pat Kandel of Jon Douglas REALTORS® in Marina del Rey, California, from their superstar status. Even though some of their prized listings had literally ceased to exist, this invincible team still managed to eke out a living by selling only $40 million worth of residential real estate. They did suffer a cut, however. The year before they had sold $60 million worth of real estate and they kept their sense of humor too. They joked that some of their listings were a little hard to find because a few of the houses had moved across the street!

Bad market, you say? Think like a pro and work the market. The fact remains that some people will still have to buy and sell. The harder it is to buy and sell, the more the public needs the expert services of a hardworking real estate agent.

*M*urphy's *L*aw

---

*I*t is usually a greater challenge for a seasoned professional to make it when the real estate market is booming because that's when all the fair-weather real estate agents come out.

They read that things are terrific in the housing market and then rush to get a real estate license or reactivate the old one. Real estate offices load up with these fair-weather licensees, and it seems that just about everyone is rushing into the real estate business to make a fast and easy fortune selling single-family residences.

In understanding your marketplace, it is important to gauge the situation in light of the volume of sales being made in proportion to the number of licensed real estate agents in your specific market area. You then adjust your selling and marketing techniques to fit the style of selling that the marketplace is dictating at the moment. Just remember: People *need housing*—the alternative of sleeping in your Chevy just doesn't work.

Step Three: Understanding
Your Immediate Marketplace

Sometimes a market will experience a switch from one kind of financing to another. In some areas you will have to become an expert in FHA or VA financing and take the time and effort to learn all facets of these loans. Other areas will require a specific knowledge of assumptions and conventional financing.

In a medium-sized city in Oregon, a very large number of agents were passed up in the marketplace because they could not or, more accurately, *would not* switch their selling skills to accommodate FHA financing. They had been very content writing conventional transactions with large down payments, but things changed, abruptly, when a number of major builders obtained the rights to build moderately priced and good-quality houses in rather large numbers. The resale market could not compete with these new homes, and the result was that if an owner wanted to sell, FHA and VA financing had to be considered. Some agents would not take the hint, and for a year or two there were some very financially fat real estate agents quietly listing and selling under this "new" form of financing.

You must use flexibility. Be able to recognize and adapt to any market that comes along. Remember that the residential real estate business is, essentially, a credit industry.

*M*urphy's *L*aw

---

*Y*ou want to be able to adapt your selling thrust to find whatever financing is needed that will enable a person to buy or sell his or her property.

That change can, sometimes, be a painful one to the real estate agent who has been stuck in a "nongrowth" selling rut for the past five or ten years.

Understand that real estate cycles will always be a fact of your listing and selling life. Make the best of them. Like anything else, the challenge will help you develop a new and brilliant facet of your abilities that would have remained untouched without the need to find another way. Welcome the challenges. Adapt to them and you will enjoy a long and prosperous career as a truly professional real estate agent.

Step Four: Develop a Daily Structure and a System To Follow

In Chapter 1, I mentioned being bewildered over the unstructured nature of the real estate sales industry and the almost complete lack of professional discipline of some agents. As with many other essentially commissioned industries, the independent contractor is the dominant form of employment. With this form of employment comes an independence that gives the vocation of real estate sales its unique flavor. There are no time clocks to punch in the typical real estate office and, aside from being associated with a loosely knit family of fellow agents held together through the bond of working for a particular real estate firm, you are pretty much on your own. You can take that long lunch hour if you want to and, in most real estate offices, you probably don't even have to schedule yourself for floor time. (Some call floor time *opportunity time.*)

If you are a licensed real estate agent, you are in business for yourself. Your office provides contact with an organized structure and services designed to help you keep abreast of the current marketplace. Most states require that you have a written agreement with your broker to split any commissions you earn so that the broker can continue providing a home base from which you can work, so to speak. Under this arrangement, it is a wonder that the whole industry doesn't collapse under its lack of discipline and isn't more messed up than it is. But it is free, and it is precisely this freedom that attracts so many talented individuals to the business.

It may attract many, but very few stay. And if you are planning on making real estate a productive and rewarding career, then you must buck the normal human tendencies to shrug off discipline and adopt those business and personal habits that allow you to be productive.

I call this *developing a structure*. It sounds simple but believe me, it is a constant challenge. Developing a structure requires the exercise of more self-discipline than most can imagine; it includes putting together a serious plan that you mean to follow. Your plan must include those important activities that lead to earning commissions and fees. Part of your planning structure will be the establishment of positive goals and the implementation of a time-management system that works for you. Part of your plan will provide for frequent scheduled days off and plenty of recreation and exercise. We won't forget the mental aspect either, and we'll be sure to make time to pursue an interesting hobby and also for a bit of continuing real estate education and professional growth. All of these aspects, and more, will be discussed in the pages of this book.

I said earlier that there are no time clocks to be punched in the typical real estate office, but now I'll add that there should be. I'm a realist, however, and I know that pipe dream will never happen. Let's look at it this way: If you were working in a factory assembly line (and you aren't, but pretend you are), there is absolutely no doubt in my mind that you would be productive. Why? Because you would have plenty of tasks to perform right in front of you and you would be required to do them or else. Period! There would be no questions asked. If you did not perform your predetermined tasks, then you would be standing in the unemployment line. Now, if we could adapt some of this discipline to the field of real estate selling, productive agents would be everywhere. But what happens in the real world is that the typical real estate agent is usually taking a break while the seriously committed agent is probably working. You know what I mean, and I am just as guilty as the rest of you—sometimes. All too often, we sit at our desks and do busy work when we should be listing, selling, negotiating or working on our files. We talk to other agents and drink too much coffee and then walk across the street to the little coffee shop and have some more coffee. Our day is an overlay of breaks and work melted together. If the truth be known (and it is), of a typical ten-hour real estate day, only four hours, and probably fewer, are spent in performing practical and productive real estate activities.

*M*urphy's *L*aw

---

*I*f you want a high quality of life and a lucrative real estate career, you want to develop that inner discipline that it takes to succeed.

We'll talk more about this subject throughout this book, so keep reading.

Chapter 3

*B*alancing Your Personal and Professional Life

*T*he idea of actually managing your time is illusionary. The real challenge is keeping your focus on the end result when your plans get second priority. Just about the time you have carefully executed and planned out a dollar-productive day, "Murphy" steps in and presents a host of other things that require your attention right now! How do you keep yourself on target? By taking the right steps with a tight focus on where you really want to end up!

The Tightrope

Now that we've explored the basic nature of the residential real estate business, let's look at the challenge of balancing your business life with your personal life. Some call this "walking the tightrope." I consider it understanding the value of your time and good time management. You can call it what you want but realize, whether you are single or very married with many strings attached, that managing time in an unstructured business is a challenge and will take a great deal of dedication and attention to achieve.

First Take: A Typical Day

Try this scenario: You are sound asleep in your warm and cozy bed when the alarm rudely disturbs the few peaceful moments you experience during your day. You bolt upright and struggle out of bed, rushing around trying to remember what day it is. Don't worry. This is normal behavior for a typical real estate agent. Family members are voicing their needs, and you feel as if others are pulling the strings of your life—and they probably are. If you are a woman, you are probably trying to decide which one of three outfits to wear and how each will make you look during the important meeting of the day while muttering to yourself about that regular exercise program you've "been meaning to start." The children are complaining (if you don't have children then there will be something else to substitute for them) that there is no bread for their lunches. Your spouse is air-drying for lack of clean towels. Actually he is more in need of an exercise program than you, but that's another subject.

If you are a man, things are still probably hectic, the only difference being that the three different outfits are two different suits, and you are probably more than a little irritated because you don't have time to shine those shoes that you were wearing when you walked through the mud during last week's rainstorm.

Frustration mounts. The car keys have disappeared. You realize your first appointment is a closing clear across town (it is a very big town), and the file is somewhere between the car, the office and your missing briefcase. It's only a few hours into Monday morning and you already feel as if it should be late Friday. What's a real estate salesperson to do?

This scene could be a common one in any household in the United States, but what makes the situation unique for you, the real estate agent, is that you are supposedly in a free business where you are your own boss. Your daily allotment of hours is supposed to belong to you, and only you. This much-touted benefit of the entrepreneurial world can, however, work against you if you lack the basic work plans and goals to maintain sanity and balance in *all* aspects of your life. "I am my own boss," you quietly mutter to yourself....

When your life and your profession have you scurrying in too many directions, it is time for drastic measures. You will have to make the break and take time for the person whom you really should have the control over—you! How is it done? By effectively scheduling time for both you *and* your career.

Where To Begin: With Time Management!

Bernard Berenson, the world-famous art critic and writer, wrote one sentence that is worth pondering, especially when we are discussing how to manage time. He wrote: "I would, if I could, stand on a busy corner, hat in hand, and beg people to throw me all their wasted hours."

For a busy person this is a heavyweight statement. For a nine-to-fiver who works at the assembly plant, it probably won't have much meaning, simply because not too much, if any, time can be wasted on an assembly line.

But in the world of the entrepreneur—and that is exactly what a real estate agent is, an entrepreneur—just think of all of those people wandering around, including you, perhaps, who do not have a clue about how to control their own day. They have no blueprint or plan to follow. They allow the ebb and flow of each business day to become a loose plan, and that means that they do not and cannot control the day: The day controls them!

Arnold Bennett, the English editor, novelist, essayist and playwright, was consumed with the idea that a person who would master the art of controlling and managing the day would be able to accomplish just about anything he or she wanted to accomplish.

Time is the inexplicable raw material of everything. With it, all is possible; without it, nothing. The supply of time is truly a daily miracle, an affair genuinely astonishing when one examines it.

You have to live on this 24 hours of daily time. Out of it you have to spin health, pleasure, money, content, respect and the evolution of your immortal soul. Its right use, its most effective use, is a matter of the highest urgency and of the most thrilling actuality.

We shall never have any more time. We have, and we have always had, all the time there is.

I have been listing and selling residential real estate for more than a few years now, and I have learned the reason most real estate agents fail in this difficult but rewarding vocation. They do not, don't know how to, will not or cannot exercise a positive and disciplined control over their working hours. Because of this, they allow their personal and family time to be invaded by their business time. The two rarely mix, and if you are planning to become a top producer, you had better learn how to guard your personal and family time, and learn right now!

*M*urphy's *L*aw

---

*I*f you don't control and manage your time, someone else will.

You must always be on the offensive when a potential thief of time confronts your well-planned schedule. That unannounced visit, that unexpected emergency, that unplanned meeting and a host of other daily events taking a minute here, a half hour there will soon consume your daily plan and your otherwise trouble-free afternoon. Make it a daily habit to set aside a block of time so you can regroup and restructure. When you have a blueprint of where you want to end up, then even the small (or large) interruptions can't destroy the long-term plan. You are able to get back on track without the loss of additional time to figure out the game plan, and you are then ready to attack the business day again!

Pretend You Have a Job

As I've said, you punch no time clocks as a real estate agent or broker, and the present managerial climate in the industry does not require a structured company discipline. In short, any real estate practitioner associated with any real estate company can leave the office at any time to run personal errands, get the car washed, visit the library or whatever. In the middle of making prospecting calls any agent can simply hang up the phone, leave the office and run to the pharmacy for that cold medicine. Nobody is going to yell at you. This, however, would not work on the assembly line, and it would be career curtains for you.

With some agents, this mixing of business tasks with personal tasks gets so extreme that every time an unpleasant business situation arises, it is avoided by running a personal or family errand. This habit can ruin productive endeavors and kill the best-planned business day.

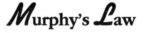

*M*urphy's *L*aw

---

*T*he key to success in an essentially unstructured business is maintaining a *discipline* and *consistency* backed up with an unfailing *tenacity*.

There is no substitute for this powerful combination. Any entrepreneur *must* master it.

Stated bluntly, you must pretend you have a *real job*. A job will, in fact, demand a discipline that few real estate agents possess, and a job will demand that you do certain things that you don't like to do. You want to develop the discipline that goes along with working a nine-to-five shift, which sometimes includes overtime.

If you refuse to play the discipline game in a typical nine-to-five job, then you will be a short-term employee. This is not true when it comes to a typical residential real estate office environment.

A recent study by the Harvard School of Business showed some very disturbing evidence: The typical real estate practitioner who claimed to have spent ten hours at the office "selling real estate" actually only spent three hours performing the tasks that were appropriate to the job.

Dollar-Productive Activities

Dr. Fred Grosse, the highly respected author and lecturer from New Zealand, has studied the top-producing salespeople in the country. He maintains that those who earn high incomes, especially in sales, have the discipline to concentrate on what he terms *dollar-productive activities*. His observation is simple. By focusing on those things that relate to adding dollars to your business while at the office and working your business day, you maintain your steadfastness in only those things that create income. Dr. Grosse calls it "staying on your business channel." That's channel 37.

The four main premises of dollar-productive activity in real estate are

1. listing,
2. selling,
3. prospecting and
4. negotiating.

If you find yourself doing busy work, you are not using the work channel to its fullest capacity. This is a great guideline for us in real estate to monitor and track our income-producing activities. If you want to make $100,000 per year, and you know that when you are really being productive your "hourly" rate is $100–$1,000, you can then calculate how many hours you will actually need to "work" to attain your goal.

This practice alleviates the guilt about being at work when you should be with the family and vice versa. When you know you have already planned the time with family and the time for work, you can really focus on your work activities, knowing that time has been allotted and saved for the real reason you are alive ... life, family and so on. Your home and personal life occupy another channel. You can only be on one channel at a time. Dr. Grosse rightly and sternly discourages channel surfing.

When you stick with the business at hand at the office and, when at home, concentrate on family matters, the balance becomes easier. It becomes normal for you to block time for life and for work. Clients and customers will fit into your schedule and you can be happier, healthier and more balanced when you have these priorities in place. There are always those occasions that demand a shift or exception in how we spend our time ... but this time, you're the one in control!

Place the Big Rocks First

In the book *First Things First,* Dr. Steven Covey explains the "big rock" theory of setting goals. He quotes a lecturer who used an example of placing rocks in a big gallon jar. Through his demonstration, it became apparent that putting the biggest rocks in the jar first made placing all the smaller pebbles and sand easier when done in the proper sequence. The same theory can be applied to taking control of our real estate life and coupling it with real life-living issues.

Human beings work far better when they can plan for scheduled activities within a reasonable time frame. For example, it is much better for you, your family and your mental well-being if you take the time to plan for and schedule your vacation well ahead of time. This way you can have something to look forward to: a goal to obtain and a pleasant thought when business pressures are bearing down.

Family and Spouse Priorities

A family night should be a regular occurrence, not a surprise when you suddenly decide to stay at home for once. This will help the kids understand that time with them is as important as career and will help you with the guilt feelings when they come up later. Consider a weekly date night with your spouse (no kids!). Take the time to plan a long weekend with just the two of you a couple of times a year. There is no point to making a lot of money and having a successful career if you are miserable in your personal life. Scheduling ensures that the event will happen and can offer your personal life the time it needs to be nurtured and healthy.

If You Break Your Body, Where Will You Live?

Your best performance at work or at home can only be expected when you feel good. Your physical well-being is important to your communication abilities both physically and emotionally. Take the time to schedule regular exercise and activity programs. This aspect of your long-term planning must (not should) be a regular occurrence and not one that you miss. If you are not likely to use a health-club membership, find something you actually like to do. Activities such as biking, blading, walking and hiking can make or break a balanced life plan.

Remember the power of compounding positive things. Even a 20-minute walk six days a week is two hours a week, eight to ten hours per month ... a good beginning. Multiply that over a lifetime, and you have a couple of years of activity! This is time that is just for you. The benefits extend way beyond keeping the body tuned up. We have a real need for quiet time, and this could provide the opportunity to center yourself in this demanding thing we call life.

Now that you have planned for your vacation time and your family time, let's continue with more important planning for your personal well-being. It is important not to work a seven-day week too often. So with this in mind, make it a point to schedule a three-

day weekend each and every quarter. Just as public school teach-
ers, postal workers, union workers and nearly every other salaried
person is granted this benefit, so should you grant yourself the
same benefit. It's not hard but it does take effort. It's easier for a
commissioned real estate agent to justify working than it is to justify taking a day or two off. It will be good for you—and productive, too!

Each month schedule a day for personal matters. Even the pope
has to get a haircut sometimes. Schedule the time for medical and
dental checkups, haircuts, massages, tax planning. You may want
to include a monthly event, like a relaxing facial or a massage. No
one will call you up and urge you to take care of yourself, so do it.
You can be of no use if you are stressed out and under constant
medical care!

"I will pretend I have a job." Don't take this statement lightly.
Discipline yourself to focus on your work channel when at work.
You will really enjoy the success.

Identify Your Time Wasters

The next step is to identify the things that rob you of productiv-
ity during your normal business workday. These thieves of time
can come in all guises and can ruin any workday if they are allowed to steal into your daily routine. Creative avoidance helps
procrastination take control of you.

Time Thief #1: Your Fellow Sales Associates

The biggest thieves of your time will be the very people you
work with every day, and they will rob you of your time every
chance they get. If you don't believe me, let's take a look at the
typical office environment.

Most real estate offices are of the bullpen variety. In this setup,
all the desks are arranged in an open room. A separate room is

usually provided for closings or conferences and, of course, the broker has a separate office. Brokers like separate rooms. It gives them a place to hide from their agents. The rest is, well, wide open.

The other kind of office is the cubicle variety. In this arrangement, all the salespeople are cloistered from one another in little cubicles or in very small, separate offices. Both configurations may or may not include a separate area for the office secretary.

The bullpen setup is the supreme time waster, but the cubicle layout is not immune to the same sort of problem. If you are in the office, bullpen or cubicle, by yourself, you will probably be able to get a number things accomplished. You will be able to work on that Comparable Market Analysis for the house up on 123 Success Street, and you may even attend to your newly created farm area or areas. But as soon as another agent walks into the office, I can almost guarantee that a time-wasting conversation will ensue. It may go a little like this:

"Hi, Terri. What'cha doin'?"

"Oh, hello, Bill. I'm pretty busy, actually, working on this CMA for the Smith house up on Success Street."

"Really? I was trying to get a listing on a property in that area a few weeks ago and, boy, I had a dickens of a time trying to find the right comparables."

And so on and so on ad infinitum.

In most cases conversations such as this will last 10 or 15 minutes, which is expensive when you calculate an hourly rate for dollar-productive activity. Unless you learn the supreme two-letter word of time management: NO. I prefer "gotta go." It's softer and often works just as well.

You'd be lucky if only one agent is in the office to steal your time. Usually there is a whole army. If you think that I am overstating this very serious time-management problem, the next time you sit down at your desk take a few moments to observe the time-management habits of your peers. You will notice a constant barrage of conversation, desk hopping, visiting and socializing that would make anyone who works a salaried job begin to wonder how anything could possibly be accomplished.

The trick is to avoid becoming a part of the typical office environment without having your time-wasting associates think you have turned into a standoffish snob. To accomplish this, you must learn that two-letter word mentioned a few paragraphs ago, NO. The word is a simple one. Learn it. Use it. You will discover the secrets of the universe, experience better health, have better sex, come to peace with your maker and who knows what else. But you don't have to be able to say the word NO in its rudimentary form. Let's go over the scene with Murph once again, only this time we will invoke a very polite and civilized application of the word NO.

"Hi, Terri. What'cha doin'?"

"Oh, hello, Bill. I'm pretty busy, on a deadline, actually; working on this CMA for the Smith house up on Success Street."

"Really. I was trying to get a listing on a property in that area a few weeks ago and, boy, I had a dickens of a time trying to find the right comparables."

"Bill, can I catch you a little later? What's a good time in about an hour?

"Great, Terri. I'll catch you later."

If Bill doesn't take the hint, and most of the time he will, then you can now insert the major time-management word.

"Bill. NO. I must get this project done *now*."

Before you run off thinking that this approach is less than courteous, let me explain that your being in the real estate business should be considered a serious endeavor. This distraction dissipates your most precious asset, your time, and it costs you money! You are not playing games. The rewards are too high if you succeed, and the failure is devastating. In short, you are not involved in a popularity contest with your fellow sales associates. You do want their respect, however, and you will soon garner that respect if you stick to your guns and refuse to allow others to interrupt you, at their whim, when you are attempting to get your work done.

A research firm on the West Coast made a study of 20 real estate offices in the Los Angeles area and came up with some very disturbing findings. In bullpen offices, the typical agent got 18 minutes of primary business tasks accomplished for every hour when more than three agents were in proximity to each other—that is, when they were in the same room with each other. In cubicle configurations, the task focus was increased to 33 minutes per hour. The main culprit for this time-wasting mania was simple. There were too many conversations between talkative agents. The next biggest time wasters were the typical office distractions such as the overhearing of telephone calls and the conversations of other agents.

Practice saying NO (or at least *later*) warmly and lovingly to all who will steal your time and, consequently, your real estate career in the name of good, friendly conversation.

Time Thief #2: Procrastination

Putting off till tomorrow what you can do today is an all-too-common practice for people in all walks of life, let alone those in the real estate industry.

Agents must exercise their own discipline. When we have to discipline ourselves from the inside and without the help of a boss, we tend to procrastinate. This is when your business plan based on dollar-productive activity really kicks in. You spend your time on your business channel doing only those things that make money. Nowhere did we say what you like to do. If you know that prospecting two hours per day will yield an average of two extra listings or buyers per week and that translates to $6,000, where is there a decision to just do it? Odds are great that your letter carrier procrastinates very little in doing the job of delivering your mail. The letter carrier is given a stack of mail to sort, and after that task is accomplished the mail is delivered. Every minute of the day is predetermined. Now look at yourself. You are in the real estate selling and listing business, and absolutely nothing is structured except perhaps the forms you use.

Management may help you by establishing "telethons" and other motivational activities, but you are the sole provider for yourself. You take the full responsibility for how much business you have, you want, you need.

The manager can only be your coach, not play the game for you.

Schedule the tasks that need doing on a regular basis. For example, if you know that you need to prospect past clients on a regular basis, block out one hour per day for phoning your past clients. This is the easiest and most pleasant type of prospecting, because you already know them, and they can give you neighborhood information for possible referrals. If you don't set the time to do a particular task, it just won't happen. Mail, phone calls and other distractions will keep your attention from those things you are postponing.

You can get up in the morning, miss your office meeting and probably not get in too much trouble, if any. You can elect to call on those For Sale By Owners (FSBOs) in your area or you can elect to make some telephone calls to those expired listings or you can elect to clean your desk. The choice is absolutely yours, and if the mood is not right, then many of you will choose to put off whatever you were planning to do until another day. Do that "putting off until another day" enough times and you will soon be putting your real estate career into the trash can. The more you avoid doing what must be done, the more you will worry about what you have not done and the less effective your real estate day will be. Procrastination will literally waste hours of your day and rob you of your peace of mind, and that will lead to wasting more time, because when you put things off they will never really be put off. They will reside in the back of your mind until a crisis is formed or the object of your procrastination fades away with the passage of time.

In order to overcome this negative mindset, you want to develop a discipline over your daily workday. You've heard the axiom "Just do it!" Well, this statement is just as true today as when it was first uttered. Do it now—or at least schedule it. You can get up off your duff and go call on those FSBOs in person or you can sit there with this unfinished chore on your mind until your whole day is ruined. You can call upon that client who is not too happy with your present level of services or you can choose to avoid the situation altogether and really ruin what little rapport you have left. You can decide to put off calling that buying prospect until tomorrow because you procrastinated about looking at the new listings that have come up for the past three days or you can get off your chair, get into your car and look at those new listings. As an independent contractor, you can procrastinate on anything and probably get away with it. But sooner or later this very bad habit will kill your real estate career.

Develop a Winner's Attitude

The difference between ordinary and extraordinary performance is that extraordinary people will do the things that ordinary people won't do. That's what makes an Olympic champion and a star performer in any field. It's never done with smoke and mirrors, tricks or shortcuts; it's done with solid basics and discipline.

The best way to eradicate procrastination from your daily routine is to develop an attitude. Develop an attitude that no matter what happens to you during the workday you will not starve to death, nor will you be murdered by one of your prospects or clients. No matter what happens during the day you will probably come home in one piece.

Now, with this attitude, how can you fail? Go ahead and knock on those FSBO doors and ask for the listing. Go ahead and call those owners who are sitting on those unwanted expired listings and truly need a professional with a plan to get their property sold. Go ahead and visit your ticked-off listing client and resolve the issues that prevail. What can happen to you?

- At the most, your listing client can vent those frustrations and kick you out. So what! You still live and breathe!
- The most your expired listing prospect can do is hang up on you. So what! You still have your ear and your mouth and your finger. Make another call. Maybe this time you will meet a nice person on the other end of the phone.
- Probably the most drastic thing your FSBO prospect can do is slam the door in your face. No problem here. In fact, the event will probably not even be recorded in the pages of history. Really! Just go back to your office and write the ogre a nice note.

Maybe, just maybe, you will wind up with something positive happening. If something positive doesn't happen, move on down the line. Next? Something good will happen sooner or later. If you procrastinate, nothing will happen.

In this world you have two choices: You can procrastinate and be miserable and broke, or you can elect not to procrastinate. You may still be miserable but probably not broke. You're in the business of self–time management and self-discipline. Selling real estate comes next. You want to develop the discipline to become a self-starter or it will be real estate curtains for you. Spare yourself the pale excuses, take your power back, make a difference, surprise yourself and go for it!

Time Thief #3: Worry

I'm not about to tell you not to worry. That's your choice. We all worry, and unless you are under the total influence of something, there will be plenty of times when you worry. The degree of worry is the issue here.

Worry is a major time waster because if you are worrying, then you cannot focus directed and serious attention on the job at hand.

Worry causes sleepless nights and the inevitable resulting fatigue. If you read your Shakespeare in high school you will know that "fatigue makes cowards of us all." Try this: Instead of worrying, doubt the doubt ... just for the hour, the minute or the day. You may be surprised at how the concern will disappear.

Other Time Stealers

Many other thieves can rob you of time. Let's list them:

- Negative attitudes
- Regret
- Fear
- Anger

It is impossible for any normal person not to experience one or more of these time-stealing emotions during a typical business day. But there are numerous ways to deal with those feelings. If any of these emotions is allowed to hang on for too long, that's when your precious productive time will be stolen.

#1: Negative Attitudes

If you are carrying a negative frame of mind around as a matter of course, it is possible that you engage in what Zig Ziegler calls "stinkin' thinkin'" or that you may need some professional help. I am a professional real estate broker, not a trained psychologist, but I do know that chronic negative attitudes can paralyze a person's productive output. I know, too, that under the laws of attraction, a negative attitude will do nothing positive and will certainly attract negative energy to you, ruining your health, relationships and eventually your career.

Negative attitudes can waste time and lose money in many ways. In some areas, well-trained, licensed agents avoid unfamiliar things such as certain financing programs. "You won't catch me selling an FHA deal," can be heard in many market areas, "there is too much red tape!" This attitude is based on ignorance, not fact. Who can't tell a story of how some lender or government agency screwed things up royally? Anyone can rationalize a negative. The negative attitude toward a certain kind of financing will disappear if the protocol of working with specialized financing is learned. Positive relationships with lenders and agency professionals can be cultivated and new rules and regulations (the government calls them guidelines) can be learned. Pretty soon you are an expert. Negative attitudes disappear when the fear is replaced with knowledge and skill. Then a new profit center or skill level is born.

How do negative attitudes waste time? In the case of the computer-resistant broker, she wastes time because she refuses to adopt a time-saving system. In the case of our FHA loan situation, time and money are lost because it takes time to work around certain deals, and it is also unethical, if not illegal. When the occasional FHA transaction is put together, the agent's lack of knowledge will waste hours and hours of time.

#2: Regret

If you are normal and approaching or passing the age of 40 something, then you no doubt harbor your share of regrets. Most of them are completely socially acceptable. But if your regrets foster a 'poor me' attitude, then you had better learn some positive ways to handle them. Regret steals productive time and energy, because the act of regretting takes over your thought processes. A great big regret session allows you only the space to dwell upon that regret. If you have ever played the "If only I" game, you know what I'm talking about. From my perspective, regret is the wrong way to respond to what should be considered great learning opportunities.

We would never have learned the lesson from the situation we are so busy regretting unless it was big and very noticeable to us. I have learned how to have a huge eraser on my pencil of life. I am now grateful for those rough spots where I made a decision I wasn't happy with later. I now know what not to do, or, if I do something differently the next time, I will probably appreciate the results later. Look at the action you regret and celebrate its occurrence in your life! Because of the incident, you have brought your thinking to a new and perhaps more productive and healthy level. There is always a lesson inside the experience; our job is to learn from it and use the lesson wisely.

The laws of attraction come into play here and there's a lesson to learn: Accept personal responsibility so you can reclaim your personal power. Embrace regret as a learning experience, then move forward on your journey to success in your personal life and in your chosen profession of real estate. You may never have learned the lesson or even become aware of the alternatives had the situation not occurred.

When it comes to real estate, you can dwell on the negative aspects of your lost listing by spending minutes and even hours in second-guessing yourself and regretting that you didn't use your listing presentation book or whatever. The ridiculous, self-defeating role-playing with yourself known as "what if-ing" is not acceptable except when used as a learning tool. And then used only once. Don't come back to it. Move on!

You can regret the investment property that you did not buy five years ago, which is worth 20 times what you could have paid for it. You can regret your lost relationship with your ex-girlfriend or the stupid things you did to destroy your marriage, but if you insist on doing such things you will only waste large blocks of time during which you will accomplish absolutely nothing. NEXT!

#3: Fear

Read any book on selling and you will find a discussion on fear. Depending upon the author, you will encounter discussions on the fear of failing, the fear of achieving, the fear of confronting, the fear of ... whatever. I am in agreement with all of these approaches to fear.

*M*urphy's *L*aw

---

*Y*our fears will impede any success you may enjoy in just about any endeavor, personal or business.

Some people absolutely will not let a personal relationship take hold and blossom because they fear the "what ifs."

If you recall, I was afraid to drive a car. It was an irrational fear. Most fears are, but they are real to the person experiencing them. They are just as real, in fact, as any physical restraint. A high fence, a pair of handcuffs, a jail—all can immobilize you. Certain fears can take the place of these physical restraints and immobilize you just as effectively.

If you are afraid of speaking in front of people, that fear can be overcome by summoning the courage to stand before a group and delivering a short talk. It's been said that if you fall off a horse, you must get back on again. It's true. Your fears must be confronted and conquered, either by yourself or with the aid and encouragement of a third party. Seek help if a fear has paralyzed you. It's never too late to overcome whatever is overcoming you.

The challenge that you are concerned with is both a test and an opportunity to learn something in another way. Don't fear it. Embrace the challenge and enjoy a new level of exhilaration called growing!

#4: Anger

When you are angry you are consumed by negative thoughts, and you can forget exercising any kind of time-management skills. Anger is a choice that you consciously make. You have to think about it to stay mad. Don't get angry. Don't get even. Just get smart—and then get on with it. Although mild anger is a normal human response to some turkey who did you wrong, it has no place in your world or the world of real estate sales. You will undoubtedly be disappointed at the outcome of some situations, and anger is a normal reaction. If you think that doing a real estate transaction consists of calling a title company and a lender and whoever else is involved and telling them "to do it" and then disappear, are you going to learn a great deal. Stock your team with professionals you can delegate to and be comfortable in knowing you are dealing with the most capable people.

Think about this as a solution. You keep your inner peace when you can just forgive in any situation. This includes forgiving ourselves as well. Have you ever said, "I was so mad at myself"? By not forgiving ourselves and others, we make a decision to keep the guilt so we can suffer. Try a little compassion. People really can only do the best they can in a given moment. It's like asking your dog to bark in Spanish—it just can't be done (yet!). Know that you have learned from the situation and are moving on positively. Accept that fact and move on.

Humor always works for me here. Finding the funny side of a situation makes the anger subside and the lesson appear. Keep your power. Laugh a little and know that you did the best with what you had at the moment, then move on....

Chapter 4

*L*earning the Secrets to Large Commissions

*H*aving identified the serious time wasters, let me say that these are all natural traits of any hardworking entrepreneurial type of human being. So relax, you are normal! Being naturally polite and allowing your fellow sales associates to take a *little* of your time here and there is okay, as are worry, procrastination, regret, fear and anger.

Being in possession of a negative attitude or two is also a normal human state from time to time. All of these varying emotional time stealers may be a bit of a challenge to control. They can be avoided, however, and the best way to avoid them is to be organized in an effective manner.

Peter Drucker, the world-renowned business consultant, coined a phrase that should be memorized and understood by all of us engaged in selling residential real estate. Dr. Drucker said:

Success does not necessarily come from **doing things right**, but from **doing right things**.

It is important that you know the difference between *effectiveness* and *efficiency*, and how these two terms can help you reduce business-related worry and maximize your scheduling of priorities.

My List

I am convinced that the reason most real estate agents fail is that they cannot exercise control over their day and they err on the side of being efficient, instead of concentrating on being effective. They try to turn their real estate world into a superorganized bureaucracy instead of a lean, mean producing machine. Over the years I have developed a set of guidelines that have helped me err on the side of focusing on the important things: listing and selling real estate and earning commissions. I call these guidelines *My List* for want of a more catchy label. It works very well for me and has been derived from a wide array of outside contributors as well as from my own input. I'll give you the list in 1,2,3 order, then discuss each item individually.

1. Always leave time for #1 (that's you!) without guilt. Set aside one hour a day for quality time for yourself. It's okay, you deserve it!
2. Make appointments with/for yourself and keep them.
3. Make a list at night of all the things you need to do the next day.
4. Do all things you hate to do first. Get them out of the way or they'll drain you.
5. Try to leave some extra time for last-minute changes. Be prepared for interruptions. Start early.
6. Create deadlines for motivation. They will keep you from procrastinating.
7. Learn to say NO! Or at least do not succumb to spontaneous decisions until you have checked that schedule.

8. Get an answering service or voice mail to ensure privacy and control of your schedule.
9. Spend 15 minutes each day for an attitude adjustment.
10. Designate specific time for personal growth. Treat yourself to additional education.

#1: Leave Time for #1

One of my favorite people in the world is Jim Newton, the author of the book *Uncommon Friends*. Jim's best friends were five people pretty important to our lives, namely, Edison, Ford, Firestone, Carrel and Lindbergh. Jim kept journals of his life with these men and wrote the book to share his insights and experiences. One of the most valuable lessons I learned from his writings was that the one common thread these powerful men shared was their daily devotion to quiet time or creative personal time.

Jim helped build the pier that Thomas Edison "fished" on while he took two to three hours of quiet time daily. Although there may not have been a hook on that fishing pole, Edison knew the tremendous value of having time to become centered and reevaluate where he was going and what he was doing. He understood the value of living life in the moment. We can learn a great deal from these writings and mirror the way these very successful people lived their lives.

*M*urphy's *L*aw

---

*Y*ou can't be of service to others when your own tank is empty.

The airlines have a great analogy I like to use about the oxygen mask. They instruct us in the event of an emergency to place our oxygen mask on first and then to be of service to others. This makes great sense, but how many of us are gasping for breath ourselves? No one will give you a call to be sure you are taking care of yourself. We can operate from a much healthier place when we are balanced, rested, enthusiastic and productive than we can if we are frustrated, overworked, exhausted and poorly nourished.

If you are a morning person, enjoy the ritual of greeting the day with a few of your favorite things. Take a walk, drink your favorite coffee in a special mug and perhaps listen to some world-class music to get your day off in the right direction. If evenings are your preference, stop booking appointments after 7 PM and enjoy the exhilaration of watching your kid play softball, taking a great bike ride or sitting in your favorite chair with a good book. This is your life, your reality. You are *entitled* to enjoy each and every moment of your existence.

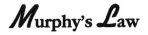

*M*urphy's *L*aw

---

*L*ife is a lavish banquet of choices, and you are the decision maker.

Take your power back and I know that you will be more fun to be around, healthier, happier and more successful in all the phases of your life that *you* choose to be.

A real estate broker in the Northwest has installed a special room in his office that is designed to be a quiet haven for any agent who wants to hide from the realities of the world for a while. It's called the fish room. This warm and comfortably appointed room is soundproofed so that the distractions of the office cannot be heard. One wall consists of the most beautiful fish tank you have even seen, and the couch is as comfortable as a couch can get. An agent who feels the need for a little stress reduction can disappear into the fish room, lie down on the couch and watch multicolored tropical fish swim lazily to and fro and listen to soft and beautiful music or peaceful waves crashing on the shore. It's an incredible calming experience.

Some people would rather take a walk in the park or maybe sit in a coffee shop sipping their favorite cup of decaf. They enjoy the conversation with their favorite waitress and like watching the people. That's why I bought a very quiet car. I can just roll up the windows, turn on my favorite CD and be completely insulated from the rest of the world. Nobody can touch me while I'm cruising in my "rolling fish room." A well-known broker in California makes it a point to ride his Harley-Davidson for an hour or so every day. The quiet rumble of the powerful V-twin engine coupled with the wind in his face offers a feeling of oneness with the countryside and creates quality time that is unequaled—at least to him.

You see, quality time for yourself can be in just about any form as long as it is legal and does not destroy your mental faculties or waste your time. President Franklin Roosevelt swam almost every day, and President Gerald Ford made it a point to practice his putting either on the golf course or at the White House. And this brings me to the second item on *My List*.

#2: Make Appointments with Yourself and Keep Them

President Ford could not have played golf or practiced putting almost every day unless it appeared on his daily appointment calendar. In order for you to experience some quality time with yourself, you must develop the discipline to schedule an appointment with yourself on your calendar and then keep your appointment. If you develop the belief that you are a valued client, then you will never miss an appointment, but if you look upon yourself as being a nuisance appointment you will, no doubt, figure out some way to wiggle out of your meeting.

You see, we all make time to do what we want to do. My broker friend in California always has the time to work on his vintage automobiles, but for some reason he had to hire a lawn maintenance service to mow the lawn. He never seemed to have quite enough time for that unsavory chore. We always make time to do what we really want to do, so let's make some time to spend with ourselves. It's really not that hard, but you may have to work diligently to keep your appointment with yourself on a daily basis.

#3: Make a List at Night of All the Things You Need To Do the Next Day

All day long you have been writing notes to yourself. You probably jotted down that luncheon meeting with your title representative and made a few notes about what you had to accomplish the next day. Now, in order to make sure that your next working day is effective, you will have to spend some time being efficient. You can do this while watching television in the evening or while working at your desk at home.

Find a system that works for you. Many people use the very popular Day Timers system, produced by a company headquartered in Allentown, Pennsylvania. This system is great for recording and logging appointments. My personal choice is the Time Design system (Agawam, Massachusetts) because it incorporates the whole act—appointments, to do's, projects and goals. This system lets me keep all of my lists in one place in a way that makes follow-up easy. Whatever system you use—the Franklin Planner, the Day Runner or a similar product—stick to it. Some successful real estate agents use a simple yellow pad or a Time-at-a-Glance book that can be found in any discount retail outlet. However, these items don't work well if you must keep daily records for the IRS or your bookkeeper. I find it best to stay with the more organized commercial time planners and organizers.

Whatever your system, make an *ABC* list. That is, make a list that allows you to control your workday in such a way that you will always be working on the most important task, at any one time, over the next most important task. Once you are finished with your most important task, you can then move on to the next most important task and so on. Your *A* list is a *must-do-today* list. If the item appears on this list, then you must do it. After all, this list should be considered a contract with yourself, and whenever you are bound contractually you are bound by your word and the sanctity of contract to perform to the very best of your ability. You will begin working on the most important item of your *must-do-today* list until one of three things happens:

1. You finish the task.
2. You are interrupted in some way. You receive an emergency phone call or you run up against a scheduled appointment such as your luncheon with the title officer. After your interruption is over, then you will immediately return to your *must-do-today* task.
3. You cannot finish the task because something is not available to allow you to finish. You may be working on an important escrow only to find that the attorney who has a key legal document cannot be reached. What to do? Nothing, really. Just move onto the next *must-do-today* task. Get back to your previous task when the attorney becomes available.

These steps will ensure that you will always be working on the most important item at any given time to the exclusion of all other items.

Your *A* or *must-do-today* list should never contain more than three items. Always check to see if they are dollar-productive activities!

Your *B* list is a *can-do-today* list. This list should be no longer than five items and should not be looked at until your top three items in the *A* list are completed. With this philosophy, you may soon find that some items on the list are put off until the next day again and again. When this happens you may find that they should never have been on your *B* list in the first place. Or maybe you will find that one of the items is really developing an importance. In that case, you may well be placing it on your *A* list the very next day. You see, this is a fluid system, and it really works if you remember to work on the most important items of the day to the exclusion of all others until one of our three things happens.

Now, our *C* or *like-to-do-today* list is the catchall list for the balance of the things you should do but probably cannot. With your *A* list (three items), your *B* list (five items) and your *C* list (the remainder of items), you will have a complete list of the things you should accomplish for the day, but if you cannot, then you will have a record of those things that you can do tomorrow. Don't be surprised to find that some items on your *B* list will be jumping up to your *A* list. In many cases the *C*'s can fall from priority as they are often not dollar-productive.

#4: Do All Those Things You Hate To Do First!

Now and then a task that you won't really want to do will rise to the top. Here is where procrastination comes into play and time will be wasted aplenty. The bottom line is to just DO IT NOW and get it over with. The real estate business is difficult enough without the ugly head of procrastination and its companions (worry and regret) following you around for the balance of the week. So screw up your courage and get that ugly thing out of the way. Call that rude client or make sure that uppity attorney gets taken care of or handle that escrow complaint. Once the problem is addressed it will probably be gone forever, and then you can recoup your energies by visiting your fish room an extra 15 minutes or so.

Setting a designated regular time to call the for sale by owner and the expired listing prospect is one of the practices followed by top producers to help them succeed. Phil Herman, a superstar agent from Dayton, Ohio, diligently calls on expired listings. His annual production exceeds more than $17 million. This is a classic example of hating to do it, doing it first, doing it well and laughing all the way to the bank!

#5: Try To Leave Some Extra Time for Last-Minute Changes

A smart real estate agent is always prepared for interruptions because the very nature of the business is interruptions.

*M*urphy's *L*aw

---

*W*e all know that the unexpected is going to happen in our real estate lives so, really, the unexpected is not the unexpected.

It's the expected, and you should make allowances for it. If you live in a large city and hope to be at a meeting that is five miles away, wouldn't it be wise to plan for a few more red lights than normal or perhaps a traffic jam? Once you arrive at your meeting, why not allow for it to last longer than you had anticipated?

If you plan to accomplish a lot at the office, you had better not plan on everything going perfectly smoothly, because the odds are that you will be interrupted in some unforeseen way ... or maybe some foreseen way. You see, you are going to develop the habit of planning for things that will inevitably get in the way of a perfect plan. And yes, getting lost on the way to a listing appointment is, sooner or later, going to happen.

#6: Create Time Pressures for Motivation

Since you are in a business where your success depends upon your being a disciplined self-starter, you can help yourself attain this success by placing a certain amount of positive pressure on yourself. Create a well thought out and arranged daily task list and assign yourself definite and certain goals that you feel are worthwhile in getting through your busy day.

One goal that all real estate agents should assign to themselves is that of gaining an evening face-to-face appointment with someone who has a need to buy and/or sell real estate. Assign this goal to yourself in addition to the daily tasks that you must perform in order to keep your real estate business on a clear and positive path. You see, an agent who is not visiting those with decided real estate needs is essentially out of business.

You may even want to let others in your office know some of your plans just to keep you on your toes. For instance, if you tell a few of your fellow agents that you plan to get a listing appointment for the evening, it will provide a little more incentive for you to practice what you were bragging about. By sharing some of your goals and aspirations with your fellow agents, you are practicing the positive art of self-discipline, which is brought about by the fear of making a bragging fool of yourself. If you let a few people know your plans and you don't accomplish them, then you could be risking your self-esteem, at least for the day, and nobody with a healthy ego wants that. Now, don't get me wrong. I don't want you walking into the office every day boring your fellow agents with constant bragging. Pretty soon you will be known as a braggart, and any positive goal reinforcement will be lost forever.

There is absolutely nothing wrong with telling those in your professional circle, and in your family, that you plan to purchase that new car on or before July with the money you intend to make by taking an extra listing each month. This is positive sharing of a worthwhile goal, as long as the goal is the result of realistic and rational thought. If you don't have the ability at your present level of expertise, or if the marketplace will not justify such production, then you had better not make such a brave public affirmation.

*M*urphy's *L*aw

*T*here is no better way of preventing procrastination than to share some of your personal business plans with those whom you respect and with those who respect you.

What I am preaching here is for you to take a calculated risk, but the risk is well worth the consequences. Go for it! You can do it!

#7: *The Art of Saying NO*

Such a little word, and sometimes so hard to say! This isn't such a challenge when you have your priorities in place. We tend to say yes when we don't have a clear picture of our life plan. If you had planned an evening with the family and someone called to schedule an appointment for the same time, you could more easily say that you are already booked for that time slot and find an alternative time to meet. Notice that because you had already marked out the time for family, recreation, study, physical exercise, date night or something else, it was much easier to make the decision to say no. Placing those big rocks first really pays off.

Know what your actual time is worth per hour, understand the full calendar of your life plan and make the assessment. Having all the facts makes it simple to make the decision to spend your most precious asset—your time!

#8: *Get an Answering Service To Ensure Privacy and Control of Your Schedule*

You have, no doubt, heard people say that they can't stand the thought of talking to an answering machine or voice mail and that they will hang up if the phone is answered by one. You may have heard it, but statistics from AT&T do not support this point of view. Whether you use an answering service, voice mail or an answering machine, it is a sound business decision. If you use it in a positive way—not to avoid calls but to exercise control over your time—you can ensure privacy and quiet time. If you understand that the purpose of the answering service is to give you more control over your time, which means ensuring a certain amount of privacy and quiet time for you in a very public business, then you will be well along the path of using modern technology to help in your real estate success.

As a busy real estate agent you will be conducting a great deal of your business using the telephone, and if you are to make lots of money you will have to deal with lots of people. Selling any product amounts to a numbers game. The more people you contact, the more business you will garner. That's true whether you are selling shoes or million-dollar homes.

The reverse is true also. You have to make yourself available for people to contact you. Many of the people who call you will want to take more than a reasonable amount of your very limited time, so you will give only those who are essential to your real estate business your answering machine phone number. By *essential* people, I am referring to important backup people such as the escrow officer or attorney, your loan officer, your termite inspector and others necessary to the success of your transactions. You must also include those who are most important to your real estate listing and selling business—the customers and clients that you need to work with on a constant basis.

I have a philosophy to share with you regarding this phone business. It is my feeling that when any commodity is free 24 hours a day, the user feels 24-hour access is normal. People will tend to call at all hours of the night, early in the morning, during dinner and any other time that is not even remotely convenient. Very few highly paid professionals are available at the drop of a hat. Because of this, I suggest that you consider not printing your personal home number on your business cards.

That does not mean to say that you wouldn't share your home phone number with those clients, customers and backup people who have special needs or who must reach you at times that are less than convenient.

Here is a classic example: My friend Linda Popp of Provident Mortgage is one of the top-producing loan officers in the country. Some years back, when refinancing was a major source of the lending business, Linda was really packing in some hours. One evening she dragged home at about 10 PM. Exhausted, she fell into bed only to have the phone ring when she was deep in sleep. A woman we will call Ms. Lee asked Linda about the progress on her refinance application. In a sleepy haze, Linda was amazingly polite and said, "Gee, Ms. Lee, I don't have your file here in bed with me, but when I get to the office in the morning, the first thing I will do is give you a call."

Linda is a very early morning person and arrives at the office about 5 AM. As promised, she called Ms. Lee at 5:11 AM and said, "I've got your file now. How can I help you?"

The moral of this story is not to teach you how to get even with anxious clients. Instead it is that Linda was responsible for giving out her private phone number, which encouraged the after-hours call. If you want to be respected for your time and expertise, consider acting like a professional and handle your calls when it is right for you. You are entitled to a personal life, family time, quiet time and even sitting down to dinner! Take your power back and reclaim control of your own telephone. Business hours (even 10–12 hours) are appropriate to take care of normal business activities. Respect yourself, your time and your family.

Consider a separate business line for your home office. This will eliminate giving out your personal home phone number. Your clients and customers will feel special if you write your "home" number on the card, as if it were not given out to just anyone. This ensures that business will stay at the office (home or otherwise). Having a separate line will also give you the opportunity to stay on your family channel while at home, and leave the business channel for when you are ready to handle it. It works for the top producers, and it can work for you!

#9: Allow 15 Minutes a Day for an Attitude Adjustment

The first item on my list is to allow one hour a day of quality time for yourself. This 15-minute respite can take place just about any time during the workday and is designed for you to have that daily talk with yourself. Just about the time that Mrs. Jones is beginning to get on your nerves with her whining about no showings of her home, or when you're getting a little edgy at the office, you may want to have your attitude tweaked. Take a 15-minute relaxation break and enjoy an attitude adjustment.

You may want to try the following:

1.   Read something that readjusts your frame of mind.
2.   Contact your mastermind or a support person to vent and re-energize.
3.   Go for a short walk.
4.   Listen to a motivational tape or your favorite music for a surefire way to get back the business frame of mind.

Whatever you do, change the scene, take a "life" break and recenter yourself.

#10: Allow Time To Grow

In my travels around the country delivering platform speeches and conducting seminars, I find there are three distinct groups of real estate practitioners attending my programs.

The first category is agents who are attending because they *have to* or have been talked into attending, usually by their managing broker. For the most part, they are nice and polite and could not care less about the educational positives that are surrounding them. In states that require continuing education, usually more than two-thirds of the audience consists of people who are taking the course only because they have to in order to renew their license.

The second category makes up about 15 percent of the audience for any educational gathering. These are the *seminar junkies*. People with this kind of personality are always looking for an educational function to attend, yet they never seem to put what they learn into practice. They may take a course on time management, but as soon as they return to the office they are as disorganized as ever. Most often they are constantly attending some sort of motivational event, yet positive changes in their behavior are seldom seen. Seminar junkies just take courses; they never implement the changes. In my travels, I have met some people who knew the subject that I was teaching better than I knew it, but they were still struggling.

Perhaps doing only one new thing a week is the answer to a new beginning in an otherwise frustrating journey. Being overwhelmed is pretty easy in the world of real estate. Putting at least one or two new ideas into practice can enable a struggling agent to start a more productive direction and help build confidence. One thing is for sure: If you are doing the same things and expecting different results, you will be disappointed. Changes in outcome need changes in direction. Be sure you put all your ideas to work before you sign up for another seminar and waste your precious time and dollars.

Now comes the positive part of this section. I've talked about the agent who attends a seminar only because it is required by the government in order to renew a license, and the agent who attends all such offerings because—who knows? Now I want to address those who are serious about getting an education and about becoming top-notch real estate agents. People in this category make up about 50 percent of the agents currently engaged in the business of listing and selling residential real estate. Here are my suggestions for making education work for your future growth and financial betterment.

Find out what areas you are weak in and then seek out classes and literature that pertain to those areas. Make a conscious effort to *apply* your newly found knowledge. If you are a terrible listing agent, then find out where a reputable seminar is being given on that subject and attend it. Model those that lead the industry in the area where you need help.

*M*urphy's *L*aw

*T*here is no need to reinvent the wheel if you find another agent who is doing the right things.

It doesn't matter if you are in New Jersey and the seminar is in San Diego; if you can afford to go, then go.

Read all the different magazine articles on how to list. Find books that relate to listing skills and read them with a pencil or highlighter in hand. Take notes, digest them and then put the principles you have learned from your study to work and don't give up. After you have devised a well thought out plan and begun to work it, keep in mind Peter Drucker's law:

Success does not necessarily come from doing things right, but from doing right things.

If you are not sure where to get your education, then talk to those in your office who are successful and have been around awhile. Get information from your broker or manager and share your thoughts about your education.

I have found that education is everywhere; however, the best practical programs are not necessarily offered by our local community colleges but, instead, by those industry leaders who travel the country speaking on a specialized area of real estate. Nationally recognized speakers and writers such as Danielle Kennedy, Howard Brinton, Dave Knox and many other legitimate experts have much to lose if they give out bogus information. They have spent years gathering and sorting out pertinent information and presenting their findings in ways that are easy to digest and accept. But they cannot make you successful—you must do that yourself. And that is usually accomplished only through your own self-discipline and focused efforts.

Somebody said that "knowledge is power," and I believe it. You are in a business that consists of earning an income only after a service is completely rendered; therefore, you must apply your knowledge before any income can be earned. Using your mind as a mental sponge is fine. But in order to earn an income now and then, you have to squeeze the sponge to render some workable knowledge.

Chapter 5

*F*arming Strategies That Increase Listings and Sales

*P*rospecting and Farming—
The Subtle Difference

Farming is always prospecting, but prospecting is not always farming. This is a subtle difference but a very important one. The trend in real estate training today is to expand the definition of farming to include working the for sale by owner and the expired listing. The reality is that these areas of short-term prospecting concern only prospects who have immediate real estate needs. Although they should be actively pursued, this activity is not farming.

In farming, the prospect base remains constant: It consists of those who have absolutely no need for a real estate professional most of the time. The odds are, however, that most of those in a preselected farm area will develop a need for the services of a real estate professional sometime in the future—some in the near future and some in the distant future.

This developing need for the services of a real estate professional and the subsequent turnover is called the *volition rate,* and it has been steadily rising over the past 20 years. In 1960, the typical owner of a marketable single-family home in any large metropolitan area would put the home up for sale after occupying it for five years and purchase a new home. In 1970, this period increased to every seven years. In 1989, the period increased to 11 years, and that makes a stronger case for a long-term farming program. The figure will vary from area to area, so check with your local board or association to get the statistics to support your marketing plan.

The vast majority of those you call upon in your daily prospecting have probably never heard your name. Don't be concerned, because this will soon change. And this is not farming, it is *cold calling*. Cold calling requires discipline to do over a long period of time, but it must be done at the beginning of your farming process and at the beginning of *any* new real estate career. To provide an example: If that expired listing is in your farm, and you have been working your farm with consistency and determination, then you will have a leg up over your competition, because you will benefit by having your name recognized and some of your services known.

One purpose of farming is to gain the lion's share of listings in your targeted area. For someone new to the residential real estate business, too much farming can lead to a short-lived career, because straight farming is only one kind of prospecting, and it takes a time investment to pay off. Therefore, at the beginning of your career, you must balance your farming activities with cold calling on those who need to sell and those whose listings have expired and left them without representation.

The nature of farming requires that you call on a large number of households that will not have an immediate need for your services and do not have even the slightest clue why you are wearing your knuckles out on their front door. You may luck out and stumble on one or two homeowners who want to do business with you just because you were banging on their front door at about the same time that they were thinking of calling a real estate agent to list their home. But most will not develop a need for your services for months or even years. It is best to balance your farming work with that of prospecting those with *immediate* real estate needs for the first two years of your career. After that, if you have farmed correctly, with consistency and tenacity, you won't have to cold call ever again. If you are a normal person, as most real estate people are, you will probably like that idea.

The Two-Thirds/One-Third Rule: Work for the Future but Don't Forget the Present

If you are new to the real estate business or if you fall within the "one year of experience 15 times" category, then you must, by necessity, focus most of your productive time on finding those who need the services of a professional real estate salesperson *now*. Your commissioned livelihood depends on it. Two-thirds of your real estate prospecting time must be spent calling on immediate-need prospects and one-third should be spent in long-term farming activities. As your farming endeavors begin to pay off, you will gradually be able to expand your farming chores until almost all of your effective time (remember our discussion of effectiveness versus efficiency?) will be spent working your farm areas. But let me give you a word of caution here.

*M*urphy's *L*aw

---

*D*on't let your need for immediate gratification get in the way of your well-planned, long-term career outlook.

Too many times I have seen real estate agents, with good intentions, begin a farming program only to let it lapse in favor of finding a hot prospect in order to earn a fast commission and pay the bills as well as the cost of Annie's piano lessons. Farming activities cease for a week or two, then begin again when the financial pressure is off. Have you ever seen a real farm that was worked only sporadically? Sure you have. Better not to begin farming if you are not going to pay constant attention to it. Farming chores must be done in small increments every day no matter what your financial, family or business pressures are.

The business of selling residential real estate is similar to any other selling profession in that once a sale is made, you must immediately move on to another sale. This is a fact of life in any selling endeavor, and it means that the search for new prospects will never cease. By cultivating a well-tended farm, your search for new prospects will be easier.

So Many Farms ... So Little Time!

The typical farm consists of a specific group of houses located in areas that appeal to a large segment of the buying public. But other kinds of farms are available. In Hawaii and in many other cities, especially on the West Coast, some very successful sales associates farm only large condominium projects. I know of one salesperson who farms only farms. That's right, this person's farm consists of farms and ranches in her rural area, and she is marvelously successful at it, too!

In Northern California there is a real estate salesperson who goes one step further and farms only those farms that grow almonds. Talk about specialization! My point is that farming need not be confined to any standard group of houses. You can work any number of residential areas. You can mix or match detached houses and condos, or you can work an area of large homes and an area of starter homes. You can even farm professions. Many agents work a list of lawyers; this is a perfectly logical group to cultivate. After all, lawyers are always dealing with clients who have to sell real estate for one reason or another, and I don't know of any lawyer who personally sells properties. If an attorney knows that you are a good, aggressive and knowledgeable real estate agent, the odds are very good that you will receive more than a few referrals.

Other fertile areas to cultivate include the following:

- Ancillary service people to our industry (in addition to attorneys), such as certified public accountants, title people, mortgage lenders, bankers (for foreclosure business)
- Real estate offices from other cities across the nation (This is where the National Association of REALTORS® conventions can give you great networking opportunities outside of your immediate franchise affiliation.)
- Real estate offices within your own city if you live in a large metropolitan area
- Clubs and organizations such as the Residential Sales Council, the Women's Council of REALTORS®, Women in Business, the Chamber-of Commerce, Rotary, church clubs, hobby clubs (wine tasting, country dancing), sports groups, biking clubs, ski clubs and so on (The list is endless!)
- Personnel offices: corporations, temporary employment services, schools, universities, etc.

The list can go on and on, but those mentioned here can prove to be a fertile field for referrals. If you belong to a franchise organization, then it will pay dividends to farm other offices within your organization.

Realities

Before you begin any farming activities, you should understand why you are embarking on this giant task in the first place. Remember, the sole reason for targeting a specific area and then calling on that specific area either in person, by telephone or through the mail is to develop recognition of your name in the context of professional and competent real estate service. This is known in the advertising business as *imprinting,* and if you are to succeed in your real estate career, you must create a great many imprints.

Because you understand the need to create an imprint on a great number of potential real estate consumers, your name will come to mind when they have a real estate need. People will take the time to call you for advice or information, and if you come across well, they will want to do business with you. If you take the time to imprint your name in the proper fashion, you will become a brand name and a respected professional in your marketing niche. Just like IBM when it comes to computers or Coca-Cola when it comes to refreshment, your name will rise to the top of the list when it comes to real estate.

Your farming endeavors will be determined largely by the turn-over rate in your market area. If the turnover rate is rapid, your farming techniques will see quicker results. If the turnover rate is rather slow, your farming must be planned for a more long-term course. According to Chicago Title Company, which conducts a study every few years, the turnover or volition rate varies a great deal from market to market. This turnover rate is calculated by dividing the total number of owned residential housing units, not apartments or government-owned projects, by the number of home sales in a given calendar year.

As mentioned before, the typical residential property experiences new ownership (a deed recording) every 11.5 years. In the state of Maine the average ownership time is 7.9 years, and in Louisiana it is a whopping 16.3 years. These figures represent a great change from the study in 1980, which suggested that the average turnover rate for the nation was 5.5 years. That figure is still being touted by real estate trainers across the country.

In the 1960s and 1970s the practice of farming was much more popular than it is now. It is important to know that, if your farming endeavors are to succeed, farming in the '90s must be practiced with larger areas for longer amounts of time.

Starting a Geographic Farm

The best farm to start with is a geographic farm or area of homes to target market. First check with your office manager about the company's policies regarding the establishment of a farm. Become aware of these policies and follow them. Don't worry about any competition from those within your office. Most of your fellow agents will not farm anyway, and chances are they probably will not be as consistent as *you* will be.

Identify Your Farm

Here's how to get started:

1. On a standard street map, clearly mark the exact boundaries of your farm area and share this map with your company's management.

2. Make sure that your selected farm area does not prohibit personal solicitation by real estate agents.

    Some condominium projects and private communities have strict rules against door-to-door solicitation. Some even have rules against telephone solicitation. If one or more of your selected areas has such ordinances, you will have to farm via direct mail. Even though such rules are common in states like Hawaii, many real estate agents farm very efficiently and effectively. If an area you have targeted has a good turnover rate, don't let a few solicitation rules get in the way of your long-term farming.

3. You are not limited to selecting one large area to farm. In fact, in many cases it is better to have your farming reflect a varied cross-section of your community. Allen Domb, the Condo King in Philadelphia, handles only one area and is incredibly successful. The negative side of having only one area is that if the market softens in the targeted area, you may suffer from the inactivity. Another issue to consider when choosing only one area is the gradual plateauing of activity. Depending on the surrounding market, the once-hot area, now aging, may be superseded by a newer development. Having smaller, varied farms may be a prudent consideration, depending on your area of the universe.

Only the marketplace will dictate the combinations available. In some cities a very well organized and disciplined real estate agent can farm one single area of 1,000 or even more properties. Generally speaking, though, it is best to break your farm up into a number of smaller targeted areas of 250 to 350 homes. The area that you work will determine the number of houses you decide to target. Sharon Falco, superstar from Roselle, Illinois, farms 10,000 homes every month! That would hardly work for small rural areas in other parts of the country. Another consideration is how varied the housing in an area is. Farming requires the strictest product knowledge, so decide on how many homes you can effectively handle in the area you choose.

By farming a number of smaller targeted areas, you will be able to control inventory that will cover a wide variety of price ranges and will appeal to a large segment of buyers. As stated before, a farm area should not be smaller than 100 contiguous properties unless a condominium or a mobile home park is the subject of your prospecting endeavors. In some states a real estate licensee cannot sell mobile homes under certain circumstances, so you had better check with your broker or manager before starting any such farming activities.

You can expand your farm by 100 homes every six months, but be careful not to take on more than you can handle. It is best to err on the side of caution and serve a smaller area very well than to try to tackle an area that will only frustrate you. The choice is yours, but don't get in over your head at the beginning. I have learned from my travels across the country that very few sales associates personally visit their farms effectively. The key word here is *personally*. There are lots of ways to contact your farm. Generally speaking, it takes 90 days to personally visit 500 homes provided that you work your farm at least three hours a day on a five-day-week basis.

Targeting Your Farming Areas

Each targeted area should contain contiguous properties that enjoy a good position in the marketplace. Each individual farm area must contain similar properties, both in price and in style, that can be financed in customary and popular ways. You want to choose properties that sell in a reasonable amount of time in relation to current market conditions and that have a reasonable turnover rate for the market conditions. All of these conditions must be met if you are to make your farm pay off in garnering sales and listings.

Select a Farm Area within the Sphere of Influence of Your Office

This is the area in which you will become famous and where you will soon develop your own private real estate sales niche.

On a map, draw a circle around your office that reflects a five-mile radius and then select an area or areas that will meet your farm criteria. If you are selling real estate in a large metropolitan area or if your office is in an out-of-the-way location, then you may have to extend this five-mile radius. Whatever the case may be, keep your farm areas as close to your office as possible. The decision will save seller objections later when you are interviewing for a listing.

Now, if you are selling real estate in a small town, the entire town may be well within the sphere of influence of your office.

Select Contiguous Properties

In most market areas, each contiguous farm should consist of more than 100 houses. In some areas this is not possible, and you must then adapt to the marketplace. I've seen successful real estate agents farm areas of 10 or 20 houses or clusters of small ranches. Whatever your marketplace dictates, do it.

Remember to keep the majority of properties in each of your farm areas similar. The word *similar* can include properties that are very much different physically but reflect a certain lifestyle, such as small horse ranches or an area of custom-built homes on various sized lots. It can also include properties that differ widely but are similarly priced.

Choose Properties with a Good Position in the Marketplace

In selecting properties that enjoy a good position in the marketplace, there are a few things to consider:

- First, search out and find a group of properties that look good and have a certain amount of curb appeal. This is only a common-sense observation, but it's worth mentioning.
- Choose areas and properties that have minimal locational objections. Marketing time is generally longer for properties with negative locational factors, such as being next to tension wires, close to a train or on a busy highway.
- Any separate farm area you select should reflect the pride of ownership that attracts potential buyers. By doing so, you will be fairly certain that you are selecting real estate that will bring a top market price and will be easier to finance and, therefore, easier to sell. They will be easier to work with in terms of inspections, appraisals, lender support and consumer demand.
- In today's bureaucratic world of inspections and federal, state and especially local government red tape, it would be wise for you to select properties that conform with the guidelines required.

Select Properties That Do Not Pose Current or Future Legal Problems

In the booming city of Simi Valley, California, a very hardworking real estate agent, at the urging of his manager, decided to cultivate a real estate farm. Being new in the business and not too familiar with the various tract areas in his community, this hardworking fellow spent a few days driving around this bedroom community of Los Angeles and, after much deliberation, finally selected a medium-sized tract of houses that seemed to be just right.

He immediately began working his territory, by the book so to speak, sending well thought out and designed advertising pieces as well as personally visiting his new farm every day or two. This activity continued for about three months until, finally, he was called to a listing appointment. He took the listing at what he considered to be a very fair price and on the very next weekend conducted an open house. As luck and some very hard work would have it, he found a buyer. Our hardworking salesperson wrote the offer to purchase subject to procuring FHA financing only to find, three weeks later, that the FHA was refusing to insure any loans in that tract because the slabs had been poured without the proper steel rebar enforcements. In short, the houses could not be sold easily under the market conditions that existed at the time.

In Wichita, Kansas, a young real estate salesperson found that her farm was rendered unproductive—useless, actually—because most of the homes in the area were in the flight path of a private airport. Not only were lenders hesitant to lend on these properties, but there were a number of lawsuits pending that scared the title-insuring agencies away.

In Kailua, Hawaii, a real estate agent spent over six months farming a very attractive condominium only to find out after writing her first offer to purchase that most lenders would not make loans on the units because there were too many non-owner occupants and the loans could not be sold on the secondary mortgage market. The only loans available were large-down-payment, high-interest packages that were designed for the investor client.

So, what can we learn from these three unfortunate experiences? We can learn to do the following:

1. Select properties that conform to the various building codes: federal, state and especially local.

2.   Select properties that can be financed with popular financing for your market area. If FHA and VA are popular financing vehicles in your community, and they are in many cities and towns across the nation, then make sure that your farm supports this kind of financing. Don't run against the norm.
3.   Make sure the properties conform to present codes. There is nothing worse than to have lost a sale because you did not do your research.

A farm area where too many houses have been added to or where garage conversions have been made may signal problems in getting the proper building permits. Be aware of these sometimes subtle signs of trouble. Be wary and make sure that your farm contains properties that will offer you and your buyer few physical and legal problems.

Select Properties That Are Similar in Price

Taking this rule seriously will help you in the long haul. Properties that are similar enough in price will make it easier and quicker for you to do the research needed for your Comparable Market Analysis (CMA) form. You want to become an expert in the neighborhood, and you do not want to have to spend too much valuable time researching every house that comes across your selling path. If you choose a specific development for your farm area, you are minimizing the amount of CMA work you will need to do. One of the newer multiple listing technology options can give us "sorting" ability for specific "models" in a particular development. This is very helpful when preparing a market analysis. To make a great presentation, consider getting copies of all the different floor plans in the development. You will not only impress the seller that you are aware of the floor plan differences, but also simplify your work for brochure presentation and other tasks.

If you are farming, as an example, 600 properties in three farm areas, it would be much better to have to learn only three basic price, floor plan and financing structures than to spend too much precious time researching 600 different and distinct parcels of real estate every time you do your comps. The best way is to prepare a market analysis in which you compare like properties with like properties, making sure that no extenuating circumstances caused the seller to sell under undue pressure or hardship. Check with the tax assessor's office, get information from your favorite appraiser, choose whatever method you want and err on the side of doing plenty of additional research and making knowledgeable comparisons. This will save valuable time and money by helping you avoid taking overpriced listings and risking your professionalism.

There are always exceptions to the rule. Some farm areas contain properties of widely varying prices, but there will be a good reason for the disparity. An example would include a farm area of small ranches or horse properties where the prices may be dictated by the size of the lots or where the houses differ widely.

The physical aspects of the property improvements may vary widely also. One house may be located on one acre and the neighboring property may consist of ten acres. A very large house may be built on a one-acre parcel and a very small house may occupy a ten-acre parcel. Although these kinds of real estate may give you headaches and fits in finding like comparables, they are really considered to be similar in the fact that they are ranchettes and serve a similar function of living, yet are really city-oriented.

Select Properties That Can Be Financed in Customary and Popular Ways

The purpose of working a farm is to take listings that will be fairly easy to sell. In the course of your real estate career, you will get your share of difficult-to-finance properties, but the majority of these properties should be outside of your farm, not in it. Because most real estate sales depend upon financing from a commercial source, your farm should be a source of easy transactions and contain properties that lenders like. Select your farm with this idea in mind.

Select Properties That Sell in a Reasonable Amount of Time for the Current Market Conditions

If you stay in the real estate business long enough, you will, no doubt, experience markets where everything sells virtually overnight! In these hot markets, multiple offers are commonplace. You will also, no doubt, experience markets where almost all properties remain on the market for long periods of time. Properties do sell, of course, but they just take longer. In Alaska and in parts of Texas, Oklahoma and Colorado, it was common to take a listing for one year or longer. This was the standard, a given fact of the marketplace. At the same time, in parts of California, a 24-hour listing was a common form of doing business. The future could bring a reverse situation. You will experience such market swings if you choose real estate as your life career.

If you select a farm area where it is taking longer for houses to sell than the average for the present market, the same will probably hold true in slow and in hot markets. Be careful here. Select a farm that reflects a reasonable turnover rate for the market conditions.

Remember, also, that expensive properties sometimes take longer to sell and that this is not usually a negative. I know of a number of real estate agents who farm only the top-of-the-market, executive homes, and they do quite well. One real estate agent in Santa Barbara sells and lists only six to ten properties a year but earns well over $1 million in income. The principle is the same whether you farm lower-end properties or upper-echelon properties. They still have sellers, they still have buyers and they still use lenders.

Select Properties with a Reasonable Turnover Rate for the Market Conditions

I mentioned, earlier, my experience in visiting Fairbanks, Alaska, and the story should help illustrate this rule. A real estate salesperson in Anchorage, Alaska, began farming in an exclusive section near the downtown area only to find out, after almost one year, that no homeowner from her farm had even called her for information. When she contacted the farm in person she was always treated by those answering the door with courtesy, and the respondents were always willing to listen and to talk. She was getting business from her other farm areas. What was wrong here? She checked with a title company and found that two houses had sold in the past 14 months and, in checking further, she found that they had not sold through a real estate company.

This small area was so desirable that when a property did come up for sale, it was purchased quickly by buyers who had contacted the sellers on their own even before the property was advertised for sale. Also, very few of these properties ever came up for sale. They were occupied mostly by old-line Alaskan families, which included the governor and other Alaskan notables. In short, the turnover rate was almost nonexistent and sales were prearranged.

This type of area is no place for anybody to farm. A number of lessons can be learned from this situation. If an area has a very low turnover rate, it will be because of one of three things:

1. It is a hot area and buyers are lined up waiting to purchase, usually without the aid of a real estate salesperson. This is rare but it does happen.
2. Something is wrong with the properties that makes them difficult to finance. These problems may include poor construction, the lack of proper building permits, legal problems affecting title and nonconforming lots. Add the problems of poor location, such as being within or near a flood plain, an earthquake zone or an area of unstable earth fill, and you may want to find another area for your farming activities.
3. The area is simply declining. This could be due to sociological problems, such as emerging crime conditions, or to chronic unemployment in the area. As a licensed real estate agent you certainly are not allowed to redline any

specific area, but at the same time you are not required to seek out and farm any area for listings that will be difficult to sell.

Your Personal Commitment

Depending on market conditions, six months is usually the minimum time required before farming activity will begin to show a small return. Please notice that I said a *small return*, because it is entirely possible that you won't see any return at all until after the first year, but you will see a return if you keep at it.

After one year, a well-cultivated farm area will begin to account for a substantial number of closed transactions. After three years, a huge percentage of your business will be derived from your farm areas.

Chapter 6

*W*ork That Open House!

*I*f you are one of the few real estate agents who do hold open houses as a regular part of your business, that's great! The distressing fact, however, is that most real estate agents hold fewer than three open house events a year, usually with absolutely no planning, discipline or focus on the long-term strategy.

Is an Open House Worth the Effort?

Open houses work very well in some market areas, but in others holding an open house can be a waste of your professional and productive time. You need to assess the reasons for the open houses, how they are received in your area and the benefits of substantial and qualified leads that result from these labor-intensive activities.

For a new agent, open houses can provide a traffic flow of prospective buyers. Some of us who have been in the business for a while don't actually sit our own open house events. This is a great time, though, to help out a new agent. I call it my "rent-a-rookie" program. It's a win-win situation that can be quite productive for all involved—namely me, the rookie and the seller.

A seasoned agent's name recognition can help a new agent. Giving the opportunity to a brand new agent to sit an open house allows the rookie to obtain much-needed new business while the seller is being helped. The experienced agent, in turn, benefits by garnering a referral fee if the new agent converts any open house prospect into a new listing or a sale and ultimately an earned commission. In addition, the experienced agent gains in the marketplace by name recognition through signs and direct mail.

If you expect to get the majority of your business from your farm areas by just knocking on doors, telephoning and sending monthly mailers, you are mistaken. The purpose of doing these things is to make the people in your *little pond* remember their *big frog*, but they won't be too inclined to give you their business when the need arises unless you can prove that you really practice what you preach. If you are "the" agent for a specific area or development, holding frequent open houses in your main farm area will give you the credibility and positioning to prove that you "walk your talk." Most agents hold an open house without understanding its dollar-productive qualities (or lack of them). Generally, the agent will hold an open for one of the following reasons:

- The seller has requested one (which makes me wonder which party has the real estate license).
- Everybody has done them for years, so they must be good for business.
- The manager "made me do it."

Here is how it is usually done and, unfortunately, it is usually an exercise in futility unless you are in a booming market, in which case just about any amateur selling technique will work.

Sally Sales is in trouble with her selling client.

"You're not showing my property enough," complains Freddie Seller. "If I don't begin seeing more action I'm going to cancel my listing and go with another company!"

Sally Sales, reacting to this kind of unwanted pressure, immediately comes up with a brilliant idea. "I'll hold an open house, Freddie, and you'll see some positive results. How does that sound to you?"

Now the pressure is off for another week and Sally can go about her business trying to make a living in the fascinating field of residential real estate. The only problem is that Freddie's house is not the right kind of property to be the subject of an open house. It is in the wrong location. Not only is it priced too high, it is generally unkempt.

Holding an open house should not—indeed, must not—be in reaction to a pending emergency or threat. The purpose of holding an open house is to find buyers and obtain more listings. It is a marketing tool and should be treated as such. Business is business, and you are not in the real estate business to waste your time on a project that may generate only marginal results.

Murphy's Law

A well-organized and -executed open house event will make you money and will increase your stature within the boundaries of your farm area.

If you follow these simple steps, you will soon be experiencing a newly found positive feeling toward this well-known (and sometimes unpopular) way of selling real estate.

Six Steps to Super-Successful Open Houses

It is necessary to adhere to these steps if you are going to hold a productive open house.

The subject property of your open house event must

1. be a nice property that has been prepared (staged) properly for the public viewing—avoid the shoddy, dirty, fixer-upper type;
2. be located in an area that people can easily find and have good visibility for signs, etc.;
3. be priced within the fair market value range according to the market;
4. support financing appropriate for that house in that neighborhood and for the current market;
5. be minus the owner for the entire open house (or anywhere close to it!); and
6. be worth a team effort between you and the seller.

If any one of these items is missing, there is a good chance that you are wasting your time. Holding an open house in the midst of your farm area profiles you as a working, aggressive agent. If you are trying to represent a pigsty as a good deal or if you find yourself in the untenable position of trying to talk potential buyers into thinking that your overpriced turkey is an exceptional investment, you will gain the respect of no one. If the house is in an area that cannot be found easily, you are minimizing the one major purpose for holding an open house—attracting numerous qualified buyers.

Now that you have the basic rules for open houses, I must caution that not all areas are suited to the open house technique. High-end resale properties are rarely open to the public; new construction built for speculation often is. In most areas of the country, public open houses are successful, but in some they perform poorly. This depends largely upon the city and the type of housing. Many large condominium and planned unit developments do not lend themselves to the open house process. You be the judge.

Holding an open house is one way of beating the zoning regulations. Each week you can be the master of your own private real estate office, and you don't even need a city business license. You can advertise your new real estate office in the newspaper and actually do business in a residential area, at least for a few hours on a Saturday or Sunday, and you can get away with it legally.

Besides that, the name exposure on your signs and directional arrows is enormous. You will be attracting both buyers and a good number of potential listing clients. You want to impress your potential listing clientele with your professionalism and expertise. That's why it is essential that all six elements of holding an open house be present when you put your time, effort and good name into hosting such an event.

Selling Yourself and Your Open House

Let's establish and accept the basic premise of holding an open house event. You are holding the open house to position yourself as the neighborhood specialist. This gives credibility to the information that you have been mailing, your personal visits and your telemarketing efforts. You are demonstrating to those in your farm area that you know how to market property. You are demonstrating to the neighborhood in a very high-profile manner that you are actively and aggressively working for those who have chosen to use your services. Don't be shy about advertising this information.

Hold Open Houses Often

To effect the profile you seek as top gun in your farm area, be sure to schedule a minimum of 15 open houses in your farm annually. This becomes easier as the listings start coming in—and they will if you keep at it with consistency and diligence!

Send Personal Invitations

At this point, you have committed to holding frequent open houses. You will need a system that is efficient in its operation and effective in getting qualified buyers and potential house sellers to attend your open houses. *Start by sending out personal invitations to your entire contiguous farm area.* Make sure that you include your photo on all advertising pieces that contain your name. Do this one full week in advance of your open house. Your best bet is to use an invitation that has been designed around your logo, style and slogan. If you are brand new and affiliated with a franchise organization, you will probably be able to find a stack of open house invitations hiding away in some unused corner of your company's storage room.

Anything can be personalized with your photo in full color! Spend the time and money to personalize whatever you mail to make it yours. Whatever you send, modify it to fortify your positioning and not the company's. Surveys have shown that there is an immediate recognition of a national logo and that your name may go unnoticed.

*M*urphy's *L*aw

*I*t is worth the time and effort to print your own personalized piece that sells you.

You will need to be consistent about the mailer you send out. This consistency should be apparent with respect to the color, style and size so that as it arrives on a regular basis, the homeowner will know without reading too much that the information is from you. A personalized postcard with your picture on the front and your customized message on the back is a powerful mailing piece and particularly well suited for use as an open house invitation. This is an important aspect of your public relations campaign. You want to be well-known, even by those who have never seen you in person. It's part of your new and continually developing positioning.

When I say that each household in your contiguous farm area will receive an invitation, I mean it. Why? Because I know of no better way for you to demonstrate to those residing in your farm that you really do what you say. An invitation to an open house is a much more effective approach to a direct mail campaign than a "blind" brochure.

Personally Invite the Neighbors

Now that your open house mailers have been sent (a full week in advance, remember?), you are going to *make a personal visit to 25 of the immediate neighbors, inviting them to attend your open house*. Depending on your market, this is an important part of your open house promotion and, again, it is a legitimate way for you to approach each homeowner with an acceptable message and not just a vague, bragging type of sales pitch. You are inviting the neighbors to attend a neighborhood event!

Your personal invitation visit should be made on the same day as your open house, just an hour or two before. It won't take long to make your rounds of 25 households. You should have an open house flyer to give to each household that answers the door. If there is no answer, just put the flyer in an area near the door where it is easy to notice, if it is permissible to do so in your market area. It's a good idea to check your local city and county regulations regarding this aspect of your open house marketing.

Personally Invite the For Sale By Owners

Next, *a personal visit to those for sale by owners (FSBOs) in your farm area is in order* as well. If you are farming a large area—say, 500 houses—you could be visiting up to ten such households. As your farming skills grow and as you cultivate your farm area over the years, this number will diminish, but for now you must contact every FSBO in your farm area. This step is critical. Can you think of a more powerful message to send a FSBO than a polite demonstration through applied action that you are really working to sell your client's home? And you'll be surprised at just how many of these FSBOs will actually attend your open house. You'll be surprised, too, at how many listings you will get over the years by using this strong prospecting technique.

If you can establish some rapport between the FSBO and yourself during this process, you will be able to ask for a favor. The dialogue could be something like this:

> "Mr. For Sale By Owner, would it be okay with you if I referred those who visit my open house to your property if my open house doesn't appeal to them? In return, would you mind sharing those who visited your open house with me? Perhaps the home I have listed might be interesting to them. Since I've already mailed flyers to the neighborhood, I'll be happy to share any overflow with you. Does that work for you?"

If you are talking to a motivated FSBO, your offer will probably be seriously considered and you may just wind up with a brand new listing.

Advertise

You've sent out your invitations and have invited 25 of the nearest neighbors to your open house and have contacted all of the FSBOs in your farm area. Even after you've made all these extra efforts, you may find that your open house is only a little better than the average open house held by a not-so-hardworking real estate agent. You're not finished yet! *To ensure the success of your open house, you've got to do a little bit of advertising.* Not much, just a little bit.

*M*urphy's *L*aw

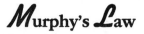

---

*Y*ou want to attract the serious buyers and not just the week-end lookers.

To do this you need to understand just how a truly serious buyer reads the real estate ads in your local newspaper. Serious buyers read the small ads all the time. They read each and every ad in the newspaper.

So, here is what you are going to do. On Monday you are going to place a very short three- or four-line ad in the real estate section, and you will place the same ad on Tuesday, Wednesday, Thursday and Friday. On the weekend you will run a larger ad in the institutional advertising section of the real estate section, and you will make sure the ad contains more white space than print.

Let's now look at how a serious buyer goes about finding a home. Let's say our fictitious buyers are Harry James and his wife Betty. They have been renting for too long and have finally made the decision to purchase a home of their own. They have been building up to this decision for some time and have done what most serious homebuyers do. They have looked at *all* the new homes in the area and have been casually visiting open houses on the weekends. They have also developed the habit of reading the newspaper's real estate want-ad section and, like all normal bargain hunters, they read each and every one of the small ads without fail, because that's where most of the FSBOs advertise. As they are carefully screening every little ad in the real estate section, whammo—they come across your open house ditty—and it's only Monday. Your ad is simple enough and reads like this:

Open House Next Saturday
1:00 to 4:00 PM
123 Success St., Anytown, USA
Hosted by Mary Smith, ABC Realty
555-5555

You can say more but you don't have to, and besides, I don't want you spending a lot of money. This is not the typical ego ad that many brokers and agents run. It is an effective ad that is designed to pull in serious buyers and a few potential listers. If you are short on cash, then run the ad on Monday, Wednesday and Friday, but do run it. We already know that Harry and Betty are going to read the real estate ads every day, and on each of those days they will be exposed to your very small but effective invitation.

When Saturday rolls around, it is certain that Harry and Betty will buy the paper and this time, in addition to your tiny ad in the reader section, you'll have a standard open house ad where it is supposed to be. It will have plenty of white space and it should be rather vague. Why? You want to attract a wide spectrum of buyers, not just those looking for a three-bedroom home with a large living room and cozy fireplace. You want to sell your open house, of course, but you also want to build a stable of qualified buyers. That's what an open house is supposed to do—attract—and that's why you are working so hard to make this one a super success.

Open House
123 Success Street
1:00 to 4:00 PM
This ranch-style beauty
offers custom features and
an affordable budget.
You'll love the location.
Your hostess: Mary Smith
ABC REALTY
657 NPQRST Blvd. 555-5555

Just picture Harry and Betty reading the paper on Saturday, pen in hand, circling all the houses they want to see, and up pops your vaguely worded but very attractive open house ad in the place it's supposed to be. There is no doubt that Harry and Betty will make it a point to take a look at your open house, as they've been acquainted with it for almost a week now!

Post Directional Arrows

When most agents hold an open house, they dutifully go down to the end of the block and poke an open house sign in the ground with an arrow pointing toward the house in question. That's it—and that's bad. But you do have to post open house signs and directional arrows. The purpose for doing this is twofold. First, directional arrows let those who are looking for an open house indeed find one, but more important, they give you a legitimate reason to approach a household demonstrating that you are a heads-up salesperson.

As I said before, most real estate agents just stick a sign in the ground and then go about their business—without approaching the property owner who owns the ground where the sign is to be placed and asking for permission. The pro approaches the property occupant and asks permission to "place a small sign" in the parkway "for about four hours" and reassurances that "the sign will do absolutely no damage to the property in question." Permission is generally granted, and the pro then invites the occupant to attend the open house, hands out a nice brochure and later sends a thank you note for the courtesy extended. If this person is not on your mailing list for some reason, be sure to add his or her name.

Most real estate agents will put only one directional arrow sign up at the end of the block, but you are going to break that rule and put up at least three, if at all possible. Why? Because you want to be able to knock on a person's door to ask permission to put up your sign and thereby make another face-to-face contact. You will also be assured of complete sign exposure for all of your marketing efforts. Let's look at what this simple Saturday or Sunday ritual will add up to if you hold 20 open houses per year, and you post an average of three directional arrow signs per open house. You've got it. You will be approaching 60 prospects per year with a meaningful contact, and you will probably be contacting some of them more than once, which will really imprint your professional image onto those nice occupants.

Flag It! With Class!

Now that you have posted your directional arrow open house signs, I suggest that you place a flag next to the sign. You want to get yourself an arsenal of those colorful triangle-shaped flags and fly them from a five- or a six-foot stake. These flags are available through most real estate sign companies.

Before you start thinking that this is a lot of bunk, a study made ten years ago backs up my position that signs accented with flags increase open house attendance. In the Los Angeles area, a large real estate firm tabulated the number of visitors attending the numerous open houses that it held. It was found that those open houses with a flag placed next to the open house directional arrow had a 30 percent greater attendance than those with just a directional arrow sign. Statistics were kept for two years, and it was a rare case indeed where a no-flag sign beat a flagged sign! (Location may have some impact on the statistics.)

An important note here: Be sure to use flags with class. Nothing can look less professional than a tattered and dirty flag flying next to a sign with your name on it. Be mindful of the area that you are working in as well. In some areas the flags will work just great and in others not at all. Make a call, and make it based on good taste and elegance!

Never Hold an Open House To Placate a Seller

If you find yourself being told how to be the agent by a homeowner, know that something is wrong with the picture. If a seller is demanding an open house, you have not done your basic homework well. The premarketing meeting is where the tone for this situation should have been clarified. Is a public open house part of your marketing strategy? If not, why are the sellers asking for one now? Do they understand how you work and if a public open house is part of your marketing philosophy? Your listing presentation should have demonstrated how you work and what you intended to do as the paid professional to market and sell their home. Take your power back and review your working agreement as discussed at the listing meeting. Holding an open house as a defensive measure is not dollar-productive!

Chapter 7

*C*reating a Winning Agent-Seller Team

*H*ave the Home Prepared for Presentation

Now that you have advertised, invited, visited, mailed and arrowed your open house, you probably realize that you've put a lot of work and preparation into your event. You don't want to have your subject property turn off any potential visitors that you have attracted. Preparing the property is the next step to an effective open house and successful showings by other agents. If you were selling your automobile, you would probably spend a whole weekend just cleaning, polishing and detailing every part of it. Your car is probably only worth a fraction of the listing price for your open house. Let's keep our priorities in order here and detail our house, for the open house event *and* general showings.

It is imperative that you obtain the seller's serious commitment to keeping the house in top condition. Until the checklist of fix-ups and clean-ups has been completed, you should not spend as much as one dime of your money or take a minute of your time and professional expertise in any marketing endeavors. The professional marketing of any residential property must work two ways. You must see to holding up your part of the bargain by using diligence in marketing, and the sellers must likewise hold up their end of the deal. That is, they must work to put their property in marketable condition.

If many things in and on the house need service, there is a good chance your seller is not willing or able to make these improvements.

$\mathcal{M}$urphy's $\mathcal{L}$aw

$\mathcal{I}$t is at your listing presentation that you will ask for the seller's commitment to either complete these items or hire someone to complete them ... BEFORE YOU BEGIN INVESTING TIME AND MONEY TO MARKET THE HOME TO THE PUBLIC.

Don't make the mistake of selling your professionalism short. If the seller is not interested in working with you to make the property as attractive and accessible as possible, you may want to do some thinking before committing your valuable time and money to this listing. There may be extenuating circumstances to account for the property's current condition. However, if your name is on that sign, the property and its condition are a reflection on your business profile.

If your sellers lack the time or inclination to get problems taken care of, refer them to a list of professional cleaners, window washers, carpet cleaners, painters and the like. This list should be carefully compiled by you from the best custodial, cleaning and painting services in town. These services have earned your trust and are prepared to work for your clients and customers on short notice. You already know that they are reasonable in their pricing, and that is another reason why they have a position on your *B* team list. Always include this *B* team list in your marketing packet.

If the screens are a mess, then rescreening is necessary. Have the homeowner get the windows washed and sparkling—everywhere! Clean, sparkling windows make the whole house seem really clean. Most serious sellers will gladly make these few spring-cleaning sacrifices if you approach them politely and with good reasoning.

Then there is the exterior to deal with.

- Are the lawns trimmed and neat?
- Are the hedges trimmed and hoses removed?
- Is the yard clear of debris?

The home must show in top form from the street, as that will be the only chance for a first impression to a prospective buyer and other agents. Your efforts will pay off in big dividends.

Now that we've worked the outside, it's time to assess the inside.

- Are the clean windows framed by dirty draperies? Then professional dry cleaning is necessary before the first showing or open house.
- Make sure that the carpets are clean and vacuumed.
- Be sure that the uncarpeted floors are spotless and shiny (if possible).

As a new agent, you may not be comfortable telling the seller what personal items should be removed or stored during the selling process. But sellers are paying for your professional insight. Be gentle about how you tell them to remove the clutter of personal items here and there. Feel confident in conveying your concern about valuables that may be sitting out in public, especially firearms, pricey collectibles and other such items. Tell, don't ask, your sellers to remove any valuables from the house and have all firearms removed from the property. You will be unable to follow everybody around who attends your open houses or be present for all showings (depending on what is customary in your area). Having the valuables removed (and whatever else the seller holds dear) minimizes worry and concern while holding the open house. As a home will show better without the distraction of too much personal property, just tell the sellers to pretend they are moving and pack up the valuables and extras!

Now that the outside and inside are equally presentable, it's time to get into some professional marketing techniques.

Let There Be Light!

When you go to any attractively merchandised department store you, as a consumer, will find well-displayed merchandise in a well-lighted, clean and pleasant atmosphere. They don't wait for you to arrive to turn on the lights and add some music. Just visit a Neiman-Marcus or a Nordstrom's department store and you will find that their merchandise is displayed in the most appropriate ways. These aspects of marketing make you, the customer, feel comfortable and make your shopping more enjoyable.

The same holds true in holding a properly planned and executed open house. The first thing to do is open all curtains and drapes and let the light shine in, if the outside view permits it. Now turn on *all* lights. If it is cool outside and the house has a fireplace (that works), then start a cozy fire. If it is hot outside, make sure the air conditioner is working.

Sounds of Sold . . .

After you have the home light and airy and have appealed to the visual senses, the next thing you have to do is prepare the aural senses. Turn on the stereo to your local easy listening station. What you want is a neutral "elevator" type of music, if at all possible. If it is not, then play something rather light, and make sure that the music permeates the entire house.

Some homes come complete with music systems in each room and that makes your job pretty easy, but most don't, so you will have to improvise. Make sure the main stereo system is on. If the seller has no music system, consider having a portable system to use during the open house. If the owners have radios, place them all on the same station, and you have low and pleasant sounds in every room of the house. Music helps the prospective buyer feel less inhibited about making comments about the home and imparts a more comfortable feeling.

The "Scent" of Success

Our sense of smell is a very powerful one, and we want to make the first whiff of this home to be a good one! We've got to make the house *smell* OK! Have you ever noticed that when you visit someone else's home it has some unfamiliar scents? All houses have their own individual aromas, and it is up to you to neutralize these different smells with a scent that is more universal. Don't expect a 500-pound airwick in the living room to help mask the negative odors of pets, tobacco, mold, etc. Nothing takes the place of clean! However, there are two additional ways to go about improving the smell of a house.

The first way to neutralize unfamiliar odors and make the open house very attractive in this department is to put a few cinnamon sticks in a pot of hot water and then brew a spot of tea. The cinnamon odor and the tea aroma are pleasing ones to everybody. Also, when an open house guest arrives, you may want to offer a cup of tea or a gourmet flavored coffee as a hospitable gesture. Old standbys have been baked bread or cookies. Keep a focus on what you are really doing here ... and it's not being a hostess but a professional. Certainly include some refreshment like iced tea or lemonade on a hot day, but keep a grip on the real thrust of what you are doing.

Second, if a home really has a bad odor, some new technical remedies using ozone can help neutralize natural organic odors through a contraption on the furnace. Check it out. Remember, nothing can match squeaky clean—a great way to start!

Sell It with a Brochure!

If you have ever visited an open house held by a typical real estate agent, you probably walked into the property only to be greeted by a very nice person intent upon giving a tour of the house. It is a wonder that some of these agents don't use bullhorns. The agent then goes on to explain each room in spite of the uncomfortable feeling that always exists between two strangers meeting for the first time. In fact, if you were looking as a typical consumer, you were probably a bit irritated that your host would not leave you alone, even for a few minutes.

As an agent, you can overcome this difficult yet typical situation by selling the highlights of the home with a detailed brochure. A brochure is the way to educate both the buyer and possibly his or her agent about what the home has to offer. Listed below are a few guidelines you may want to consider when designing your brochures.

The handout should help prospects learn all the fine points about the home so you aren't following them around pointing things out. Although tagging items can sometimes work, if the home has a lot of upgrades, this technique may look tacky, and you'll have to hope the kids don't move the tags. Having the brochure do it for you gives prospects some solid information to peruse later as well. To help the recall of the home start with the following:

1. **A color photo of the exterior of the property**.
    This is easy to do. Just load some film in your camera and take some snapshots. There should be a full picture of the front and, if the property permits, two or three interesting interior shots. You can simply paste your color photos on a sheet of standard or legal size paper and type captions below the pictures with your computer. After you fill in the rest of the details (as we will cover shortly), you can then throw your original on the copy machine and you will have a very presentable, informative brochure.

Or you can plan, plan, plan and have a professional printer do the job. This is your choice. But be careful not to get too efficient here. You don't want to wind up in the brochure business, although I know of one real estate agent who did and now owns his own print shop, which caters almost exclusively to the needs of real estate salespeople.

2. **A section containing the statistics of the property.** This section can reflect some of the information contained in your Multiple Listing Book. These items should be mentioned:

- **Price**
- **Address**   As recognized by the Post Office
- **Lot size**   Make sure that you are accurate in determining lot size; check with your local tax assessor and perhaps include a copy of the last survey.
- **Square feet**   Sometimes this information is available through the tax assessor's office. If you asterisk this section and print a disclaimer near the bottom of your brochure, such as "This figure is an estimate only and must be verified by any potential purchaser prior to purchase," you'll be covered just fine.
- **Baths**   Remember that a full bath contains a tub, a sink and a toilet. If there is a shower over the tub, then it is still just a full bath. A 3/4 bath contains a sink, a shower and a toilet. A 1/2 bath contains a sink and a toilet. You should not just say "three baths" if the property, in fact, has only one full bath and two 3/4 baths. Instead enter 1 + 3/4 + 3/4. That's the professional way.
- **Year built**   In some areas the tax assessor has this information; if not, use an approximate year and then say so.
- **Foundation**   Slab, raised, pier, etc. *Be accurate.*
- **Roof**   Asphalt, cedar, tile
- **Patio**   Is it covered or open? Cement, aggregate? Features?
- **Siding**   Wood, vinyl, stucco, aluminum?

- **Landscaping**   What about built-in sprinklers, exotic plants, unusual trees?
- **Flooring**   Is there hardwood under those carpets? Be careful here, and don't rely on the representations of the seller. You don't want a lawsuit later! Have the carpeting and padding been upgraded?
- **Heating**   Forced air, baseboard, natural gas, propane, coal?
- **Cooling**   Refrigerated, sump, fan?
- **Bedrooms**   State the number and give the dimensions. Remember, for a bedroom to be legal for FHA or VA and most other forms of financing, it must have a closet and be entered from a neutral room such as a hallway.
- **Living room**   State the dimensions.
- **Dining area**   State the dimensions. Formal?
- **Kitchen**   State the dimensions. Gas, electric? Features?
- **Laundry**   Where is it? Gas, electric? Features?
- **Schools**   Name them—elementary, junior high, high school.
- **Terms**   If any. If you are working your power team, you might have your lender do a finance options spreadsheet for this home. You might include if the property is built to FHA/VA standards and qualifies for government financing.
- **Comments**   In this section you want to mention the items of interest that have not yet been mentioned.

    You may want to include comments on several special features in the home that are not easily visible. Extra insulation, newer roof, fully wired theater sound systems, underground utilities and sprinklers are just some of the hidden features that can add value and desirability to your open house. Updated heating, cooling and plumbing systems and new roofing are other items of high interest to a prospective buyer.
- **Special upgrades**   If the home is part of a tract development, highlighting the special upgrades may distin-

guish it from other similar models competing in the marketplace. Upgraded frontal elevations, premium lot size and location, professional landscaping and decorating all can help you sell the home to an interested buyer.

- **Inclusions and exclusions from the sale** The brochure is a great place to be specific about what items the seller intends to include in the sale. This informs the prospective buyer (and the buyer's agent) if the crystal chandelier in the dining room is included or if a credit will be given. Appliances are usually another issue; what is included must be clarified. In some areas of the country, certain appliances are always included. At the listing interview, determine the seller's intentions and communicate them to the buying public through your brochure. Making these issues clear before the contract is drawn can help prevent complications later.

The Wrap-up

You now have a home that is easy to find, clean, well lighted, pleasant sounding, nice smelling and self-explanatory. Even if it doesn't sell during the open house event, you will have succeeded in impressing those who have visited from your farm, and you certainly will have impressed potential buyers and sellers with your professional presentation and marketing strategies. You'll be surprised at how holding a series of these open houses reflects positively on your professional reputation.

Sign-in Book?

You may have noticed that I have not included a sign-in book for the open house. Let's consider this item as an option because, in my opinion, it can have an inhibiting effect on a visitor who is not interested in giving out a name, address and phone number to a stranger in a strange house. Many times open house visitors will refuse to sign the register, and if that happens, as it frequently will, you probably now have created some subtle tensions in the mind of your guest.

Many times, also, a visitor will sign the register but will feel somewhat uncomfortable about it. How do I know? I have no proof except the conversations I have had with those who have attended open houses and were "forced" to fill in some sort of sign-in book.

When a visitor does arrive, you may pick up some buying signals, and then naturally, at the appropriate time, strike up a conversation with that person. You will probably get a name and phone number if you use an approach similar to this:

> **Agent:** "Hello, I'm glad you could attend my open house. Tell me, did you find out about it from the newspaper or from my open house signs?"
>
> **Prospect:** "Well, neither. We received one of your invitations in the mail."
>
> **Agent:** "Then you live in the area. Why don't you just look around and make yourself at home. I've got some fresh coffee. Would you like a cup?"
>
> **Prospect:** "No. Thank you."
>
> **Agent:** "Just make yourself at home. If you should have any questions, please ask."

Let the prospect wander for a few minutes. (Don't worry. Nothing terrible is going to happen.) Then casually approach the prospect and engage him or her in some kind of small talk. You may want to point out a special feature in the bathroom, such as the adjustable shower head or the large vanity with lots of drawers and storage space. Then say: "By the way" (an excellent phrase to use when you want to change the subject), "are you going to sell your present home before you buy a new one?"

By using this trial balloon closing question, you will quickly find out if you are dealing with a homeowner who is using your open house to get a comparable. I have found that more than half of my open house visitors are really listing prospects who are just using the open house market as a vehicle to gauge how their house will fare in the resale arena. Most real estate agents automatically treat them as potential buyers. Don't fall into this trap. Find out early if you are dealing with a potential listing client or a potential buyer.

> **Prospect:** "No, we are just looking right now."
> **Agent:** "Great. I understand. Have you been looking for a home very long?"
> **Prospect:** "A couple of weeks now. This is a nice home. How much is it?"
> **Agent:** "That information is mentioned in my brochure. Here is a copy. By the way, Mr. Prospect, my name is Terri Murphy, and yours?" (A close this blunt, if offered within the context of a casual conversation, will work almost all the time.)
> **Prospect:** "Oh, I'm Harry and this is my wife, Betty."
> **Agent:** "Glad to meet you, Harry and Betty. Here is my business card. You know, if you want up-to-date information on homes in this area I can add you to my 30-day mailing list, and I'll send you information on what is coming up for sale in the next 30 days. After 30 days, I will need your authorization to continue updating you. Where should I mail those updates?"
> **Prospect:** "Well, I don't know. Why don't I just call you?"
> **Agent:** "That's fine, but what I am hearing is that you don't want me or any other salesperson to invade your privacy and I understand. I do consider myself a professional in the real estate business and if I can be of any assistance to you, I'm happy to help. I can mail you very pertinent and accurate information as it becomes available when you're interested."
> **Prospect:** "Well, maybe you can."
> **Agent:** "Where will I mail it?"
> **Prospect:** "OK. It's 123 Success Street, right here in Golden City."

Agent: "Thanks, Harry. If a really special property comes on the market that meets your specifications, would you prefer that I call you? Where should I call?" (If the answer is yes, you will easily gain the prospect's telephone number. If the answer is no, all is not lost. You can simply mail the prospect an informative brochure along with a friendly letter.)

Prospect: "Well, I don't know. Why don't you just send me the information."

Agent: "Will do, Harry." (Hey, you can't win them all, and at least you've got the mailing address.)

Now go on with the showing process and, who knows, maybe at the end of the open house tour Harry and Betty will have opened up some more and have begun to accept you as a real estate professional. The chances are you will get their phone number in another ten minutes or so, and you may even get an appointment to show other properties or even list their home. After all, you are an impressive salesperson. Your open house event proves it!

Have a Backup

Suppose that you truly luck out and Harry and Betty indicate that they are really looking hard for a house and have to buy soon. They are from out of town and have taken this weekend to do some serious shopping, and they figured that the best way to begin their search was to take a look at some open houses. Most new buyers begin their search for a home by first driving around and scoping out the neighborhoods, then by reading the newspaper ads and then by attending open houses. You have two possibilities here.

Plan A is really no plan at all. You can say something dumb, like "Well, Harry and Betty, I'm stuck here until 4:30," or you can have a backup plan to help you assist them now. To keep them from finding another real estate agent or looking at open houses until they stumble upon one they like, have a Plan B.

Plan B is in gear when you walk over to the phone, call your prearranged backup and say something like "Hi, Mary. This is Terri. I've got a good prospect here who wants to look at more properties." Mary knows what to do. She will be at your open house in ten minutes or less. If she should luck out and sell it while you are out with Harry and Betty, then you will be responsible for paying her any commission split that you had prearranged with her.

Now, let's get real here. You don't want to have planned, advertised and executed a complicated open house strategy like that outlined in this chapter and then just leave it.

*M*urphys *L*aw

Definitely have a prearranged backup ready to either take over your open house or show the properties for you on short notice.

If you have not arranged for a backup, then don't leave the open house. It would not be fair to your open house client or to those members of the public who have planned on attending your well-orchestrated event.

The Right Price

I also mentioned that the property should be priced within the market and I mean exactly that. Here's why. Just as soon as you hold an open house for an overpriced property, that will be the exact day a listing prospect from down the street who owns a very similar house will wander in. If you have your open house up for $185,000 and it's really worth a top dollar of $160,000, then you will find yourself in a real live Catch 22 (read the book!) when your prospect invites you to look at his house that evening. If you do get the listing, you will now have two overpriced houses for sale in the middle of your farm, and that's not good.

Those of you who have been in the business for a while all know of some real estate agent in your Multiple Listing Service who always lists properties too high or with bad financing or some other problem. Watch it! Once you get that reputation, it is very hard to dump it. That's why your open house events must have these very fair but restrictive parameters. Which brings me up to my fourth point. Again!

If you hold an open house that cannot support financing that will appeal to the majority of the buying public, then what apology are you going to make to the interested buyer who wants to buy and you can't deliver? No financing, no open house. That's a rule. Follow it.

Send the Owners Out To Play

The owner must be completely out of the house along with the dog. If a potential buyer of your open house knows that the seller is within earshot, then you will not be able to have a real conversation. The potential buyer will, quite naturally, hold back in asking questions or offering criticisms of the property, which always happens in the very early stages of the buying process.

Some owners find it difficult to stay out of the way; and it is a natural tendency for any owner to want to become part of the showing process and override the leadership of the real estate agent. The owner must be out of the house.

Chapter 8

*P*ower Prospecting
Secrets

*W*e have talked about Peter Drucker and his very clever play
on words:

> Success does not necessarily come from doing things right,
> but from doing right things.

Doing a "right thing" not only entails working on your immediate
tasks and daily endeavors, it also includes a long-term commitment to, and an understanding of, the concept of prospecting. It
means working with a great number of people who, when it comes
to buying and/or selling real estate, think of you as *the* professional to contact. The only major difference between the average
real estate agent and the superior real estate agent can be stated in
one word—*prospector*. Top-producing real estate agents are *always* prospecting for new business. They are constantly looking,
looking, looking for new buyers and sellers. They never stop. It's
an obsession.

What Is Prospecting?

Prospecting is also the act of seeking out and approaching those who may have an immediate need for your real estate services. We covered this aspect of prospecting in our discussions of the for sale by owner, the expired listing, holding an open house and farming. Although the vast majority of successful real estate agents prospect in these areas, they are by no means the only ones. In fact, so many ways exist to prospect for potential buyers and sellers that a whole book could be written on the subject. This chapter will give you some tried-and-true ways to prospect that work very effectively. In short, these prospecting methods are probably not being used a lot in your market area and are just waiting for a real professional to implement them.

Keep Your Name in the Mirror

Your local newspaper is the mirror of the community and, as such, is the publication that gives the prospecting agent leads to people who have, or who will soon have, a real estate need. The following story illustrates an important point. It is a true narration of what happened to a real estate agent in Tennessee.

Every morning Frank would sit quietly at the breakfast table and read the local newspaper, but this is not unusual. It is done every day by people from all walks of life. The difference with Frank was that he read the newspaper with a felt-tipped pen in his hand and a legal-size notepad by his side. When he came across an article that told of a person receiving a promotion or taking a new job in the community, Frank would note this on his pad and cut the article out of the newspaper.

One morning Frank noticed that the city had just hired a new fire chief. The new chief, who was going to assume his duties the following month, would be moving to Frank's community from a neighboring city. Later, at the office, Frank found the address of the new fire chief by using an out-of-town telephone book obtained from the local library. Frank then wrote the new fire chief a nice but businesslike letter introducing himself and his real estate firm. With the letter Frank enclosed the article that had appeared in the newspaper that morning. After a few days, Frank called the fire chief. A few weeks later Frank sold a home to the fire chief. Frank also referred the fire chief to a real estate agent in the neighboring city and received a referral fee for the service. When the fire chief was asked how many other salespeople had called on him, he replied that no other real estate agents had contacted him. He was contacted by two insurance agents, however, and a stockbroker.

It is interesting to note that Frank makes at least three sales per year by using this prospecting method, and he also lists anywhere from two to seven homes each year. Also, Frank has never run across any other salesperson using this method of prospecting. He is absolutely alone and free of competition in this area.

As Frank's case illustrated, the newspaper can be a very fertile area for prospecting. Most real estate agents call on expired listings, and many agents cold call by phone and by door-knocking as well, but very few use the newspaper as a prospecting vehicle. The next time you pick up a local newspaper, take some time and search for prospecting leads. They are numerous and they are fun to pursue.

The For Sale By Owner (FSBO) Ads

The for sale by owner advertisement is the best source of listing prospects that can be found. You will probably find yourself bucking quite a bit of competition from other real estate agents, but you will find that very few of them will offer permanent competition. Some will prospect the real estate ads for a week or two, then drop out for a few months and return again only when their economic situation dictates. This will be a short-lived marketing strategy, however, and things will soon return to the status quo. If you stay with this mode of prospecting with consistency, over the span of your career you will quickly become the dominant force in listing the FSBOs advertised in the newspaper.

Competition in this area is great because the for sale by owner ad jumps out and begs the typical real estate agent to call—at least sporadically. The FSBO ad is, in a sense, an advertisement for help. If you are going to pursue the FSBO, please remember that this seller has probably been contacted by a large number of real estate agents possessing varying skills. By the time the FSBO gets your call he or she may be a little on edge, to say the least, and probably somewhat putout with real estate salespeople in general.

*M*urphy's *L*aw

*T*he way to contact the FSBO is to be more professional than your competition.

Your competition has been calling on the telephone. You may want to pay a personal visit and follow that visit with a sincerely written thank you note. The professional salesperson knows that the easiest way for a client prospect to say no is to say it over the phone. Saying no to a well-dressed and pleasant professional in a face-to-face situation is a little more difficult.

Most communities have a criss-cross directory that will quickly give you the name of the person whose home is advertised for sale. By knowing the prospect's name, you are armed with a valuable weapon to help you break the initial defense barrier all prospects use as a shield when meeting a salesperson for the first time. How you introduce yourself is entirely a matter of your own personality and will not be discussed here. The purpose of this chapter is to acquaint you with prospecting sources, not sales techniques and closes as such.

*M*urphy's *L*aw

*N*ever ask a prospect to list his or her home with your company on the first visit.

The purpose of the first visit is to soften the defense barrier, as previously discussed, and to introduce yourself to the prospect. You want to make the FSBO feel that you are there to help. Perhaps you can discuss general real estate trends in the area or offer advice on financing. It's not a bad or a pushy thing to ask to see the interior of the FSBO's home. After all, you make your living selling residential real estate, and knowing what is on the market is part of your job description.

You can say something like this:

"Mr. Smith, in my everyday duties as a real estate agent I look at a number of houses in this area. This helps me keep abreast of the current real estate market. Would you be offended if I took a quick look through your house?"

(Do not hesitate after this sentence but go right ahead into the next sentence.)

"By doing so you will be helping me stay current with what is being offered for sale here in Walnut Creek and, at the same time, I may be able to give you some ideas that will help you sell your house quickly."

Most of the time you will receive a reluctant "Yes," but you must first ask. Remember, if you don't ask, then you don't get. Lots of turn-of-the-century salesmen had that statement prominently posted over their desk or carried in their briefcase. Do not suggest a price until you have thoroughly inspected the home. After you have inspected the property, go back to your office and make out a complete Competitive Market Analysis. This form will give your prospect a sample of your professionalism, and you will eliminate any guesswork as far as pricing is concerned. It will also give you the logical and acceptable excuse to make another appointment with the FSBO.

The For Rent Ad

For Rent ads are plentiful in any local newspaper, but they are frequently overlooked as an excellent listing source. Often the owner of the rental property is weary of putting up with the hassle of having a rental, and many such owners are looking for an excuse to sell their misplaced investments. They would love to have some real estate salesperson coax them into listing their property for sale.

People who have rental properties frequently are real estate investors who own a great many such properties. Sooner or later this kind of prospect will either buy or sell.

*M*urphy's *L*aw

---

*I*t is inevitable; if you cultivate the landlord as a client, you will soon reap an abundant harvest of real estate commissions.

Again, many successful real estate agents spend much of their prospecting time getting to know a large number of landlords and apartment house managers. The newspaper is the place to start this kind of prospecting.

The Trust Deed for Sale Ad

Every local newspaper has a Trust Deed column in the classified advertising section. This is where people advertise their private real estate mortgages for sale or advertise to purchase trust deeds or mortgages. The people who place these ads are very real estate–minded and are usually more affluent than the average prospect.

Whether these prospects have a real estate need is really not too important to the professional prospector. The important aspect here is that they are a source of referrals. Because they are real estate–oriented, it is only logical to assume that they know a number of other people who have real estate needs. Not only are these prospects good for real estate referrals, they can also be a viable source of financing. As a professional prospector, you should always have three or more trust deed and mortgage investors in your stable of potential business prospects.

The Garage Sale Ad

Recently, garage sales have become very popular in residential America. It is not unusual to find that a garage sale precedes a house sale. A recent study made in a suburb of Wichita, Kansas, found that 20 percent of all families holding a garage sale placed their home on the market within 30 days after the garage sale. This is indeed a startling statistic, yet very few real estate agents even bother to call on the family that is holding a garage sale. Even if you cannot get a listing from a garage sale lead, it is an excellent place to advertise that you are in the real estate profession.

Many companies offer garage sale kits, including free signs, to people who want to hold a garage sale. The only addition to the signs is a statement directly under the words *Garage Sale* bearing the name of the company.

"Compliments of ABC Realty"

The agent takes these garage sale signs to the prospect and offers them as a service. It is a terrific advertising technique, and many times it leads to a listing or a sale contact.

Help Wanted Ads

The professional prospector can obtain a number of excellent prospect leads by contacting employers. Many times an employer will hire an employee from out of the area. The real estate agent who develops a relationship with a local personnel department will soon be richly endowed with many good prospect leads.

Birth Announcements

Scanning this part of the newspaper can be a rewarding experience when it comes to earning future commissions. Most of the time the address of the new parents is not given, but it is relatively easy to find the property's address and the phone number in the criss-cross directory or in the phone book. In calling upon the new-parent prospects, be sensitive to the adjustment they have to make with a new baby in the home. It is not uncommon for new parents to be inundated by dozens of salespeople of one type of another.

Perhaps a note of congratulations immediately after reading the birth announcement is in order. Wait a month or two and then write a note of introduction. A personal visit can follow a few weeks later. Remember, your duty as a professional is to provide a service for your clients, and a growing family often heralds the need for a larger home. Be considerate and very careful in your conduct and you and the new parents will benefit from your mutual acquaintance.

Public Notices

Each day the newspaper is filled with notices of a legal nature. The law requires a person to file a notice when entering into a business or a partnership. It also requires a notice when a person abandons a partnership or fictitious name. These notices can signify that a person has, or is going to have, a serious real estate need. If a Notice of Dissolution of Continuation of Business has been filed, the real estate professional may well have an exceptional listing lead. Perhaps a lead for a commercial lease can even materialize! If a business is about to close, the landlord will need a new tenant and the services of a good real estate agent.

Many times, when a businessperson files for a dissolution of a business, it does not mean that there is a negative business problem. There may be only a restructuring of the business, the buyout of a partner or the addition of a new partner. Take your time to read through these notices, then do a little follow-up work. It can lead to great rewards.

Many other kinds of public notices are published daily in your local newspaper. Each kind, from a bankruptcy notice to a notice of foreclosure, may be a disguised advertisement for a pending real estate need that has to be satisfied, and no public notice should be overlooked. When prospecting the public notice section, however, please be considerate of the prospective client. Many times, as in the case of a new parent, the party is under considerable stress and strain. In the case of a pending bankruptcy, if an attorney is involved, as will be the case most of the time, it may be better to contact the attorney. Use discretion. A good idea is to begin each initial contact with a well-written letter. Try to avoid telephone contact until the prospect has had time to be introduced to you through your written contact.

Enlisting a Good *B* Team

This is another excellent listing and selling prospecting source. When you refer business to other service-oriented businesses that work in the real estate industry, you can prospect for referrals. A good example is working with a local decorator. If you should list a property that is new construction, essentially a "vanilla box," consider working with a professional decorator. You can ask the company to design a "decorator board" to be displayed on an easel in the listed property. The board will show an array of fabrics, colors, swatches of carpeting or materials, and ideas for window coverings in a display format to give prospective buyers an idea of how they might decorate their new home. The bottom of the board says:

"Made especially for Agent Annie by Designs & Decorators."

This is a natural way to prospect and refer back and forth between spheres of consumers and influence. A prospective buyer is likely to call the decorator for tips on decorating the home or ordering window treatments after buying the home. The decorator returns the favor by referring the agent when called to help update the look of a home from a homeowner interested in getting it prepared to sell.

Other B team prospecting exchanges can be done with a myriad of services to which you refer, and hopefully they will return the favor. Cleaning services, landscapers, maintenance services ... the list is endless! By getting to know a few handymen and yard maintenance services in your community, you can have an advance source of information about whether other people are going to move. These people are constantly working in various parts of the community. They can act as extraordinary "bird dogs" for the professional prospector.

Indirect Prospecting

The examples we have discussed are direct prospecting from newspaper and professional sources. Indirect prospecting is another technique that works, but the results are not immediately apparent.

Indirect prospecting takes place when a child is mentioned in a newspaper article or an article is written about the local high school band winning a musical contest. In cases such as these, the professional prospector would write a very nice note of congratulations and then wait for quite a while. After a few months, the prospector would then send a "remembering" card or another friendly note. What is important here is that the parents and the band director will feel honored by the kind gesture on the part of Mr./Ms. Professional Prospector. You can be assured that these people will remember that thoughtful real estate agent when it comes time to fulfill their real estate needs.

Prospecting and Relocation

Transferees are often assisted by a relocation company or executive assistance programs through different service companies contracted by their employer. If you are interested in getting a higher profile in the relocation arena, consider attending the national conventions and seminars sponsored across the country. Several different associations now offer designations that certify you as a relocation specialist.

Not all large companies contract with just one real estate company to handle their executive transfers. Put together your promotional package and arrange to be interviewed by the appropriate company officer. Have testimonial letters from other families you have helped through the transition phase. Be ready to assist relocating employees coming to your area and reap the rewards!

Builders, Anyone?

Another great source of listing and buyer prospects is your local building community. If you are in an area that enjoys development and a healthy amount of new construction, prospecting the builders may add to your business. For example, a builder may contract with a family to build them a new home. If the builder is sold on your professional and aggressive marketing, that builder can refer the sale of the buyer's present home to you for a smooth transition!

Some builders will share their sign-in sheets with real estate agents if they do a lot of business together. They know that the agent who contacts prospects can sell them on the builder's product and also list their home for sale. And selling the existing home enables them to buy the new construction. Don't pass up the opportunity to work those leads. Become a member of the local homebuilders' association for higher visibility. Let builders know that you refer them to those prospects who ask you for new construction. Make this a win-win situation for all involved for maximum success!

Prospecting becomes a way of doing business naturally every day. It makes good sense to help those who help you, and vice versa. Prospecting has a way of working in your best interest when you work it into your daily routine. It pays off when you least expect it!

Chapter 9

*M*arketing Yourself as *the* Industry Expert

"The goal of marketing is to make personal selling obsolete."
— *Peter F. Drucker*

*N*etworking is the delicate art of building mutually beneficial relationships for long-term, continuous business flow. It is an essential element to any service professional interested in long-term results and in working smarter, not harder. When you combine networking with a focused plan for personal marketing, your networking efforts have more impact and a higher profile.

It makes good sense to tap into your already rich resource bank of affiliates, past customers and ancillary services to create a win-win situation with people who share your commitment to serving others.

One of the foremost speakers and authors on the art of networking is Bob Burg, of Burg Communications in Jupiter, Florida. In his book *Endless Referrals*, Bob tells us that

"networking for a profit is the building and cultivating of a large and diverse group of people who will gladly and continually refer you business.... The real key is to get as many people as possible to feel as though they know you, like you and trust you. It's like creating 'walking emissaries' of good will."

Successful salespeople understand the value of carefully investing the time to nurture auxiliary relationships for building a strong foundation to a growing business and long-term career. To be effective, this can only be accomplished with a marketing plan coupled with a marketing strategy.

The plan need not be complicated. It's like farming or any other strategic plan. Any good plan has one basic secret: It takes consistent steps and personalization to give you optimum results.

What's Your Plan?

*M*urphy's *L*aw

---

*T*o be effective at networking, you must create a personal marketing plan of action—a specific, step-by-step strategy to develop a high profile and to nurture your contacts, which will maximize your efforts.

These steps include the following:

1. Identifying your area of specialization
2. Identifying your niche
3. Combining your specialization with a personal interest
4. Developing a marketing program that includes a personalized logo, slogan, theme and color to heighten personal identification
5. Developing marketing pieces for specifically targeted groups
6. Implementing a long-term annual strategy for customer/client contact using varied avenues of communication
7. Planning strategic events to solidify relationships of a personal level in a social atmosphere with an emphasis on the "personal" aspect

8. Getting up to speed with technology
9. Developing and implementing a highly personalized system of acknowledgment for those people who send you referrals
10. Using personal marketing in your prelisting packet

Marketing helps customers and clients think of you when they identify a need for your service. Somehow, they have to be able to find you in the sea of able professionals. It's not as though they have been studying the newspapers on a regular basis, either. It's a need basis, and they will be aware only when the need presents itself.

This first step necessary to building your network is to give those contacts help in "finding" you. To avoid diluting your efforts, consider targeting a particular segment for maximum visibility. The first decision is the area in which you prefer to build an abundance of contacts. This effort is magnified by a plan of action.

Step #1: Finding Your Specialization

A great example of specialization is the Star Power producer, Allan Domb, of Philadelphia. Allan is the "Condo King" of the Philly area. He specializes in a particular group of condominiums with a six-square-mile radius.

Allan is a $50 million plus producer annually. He knows better than to do anything else but this chosen condominium market. He knows his highest dollar-productive activity comes from sticking where he knows the terrain. Allan refers out all single-family prospects that he gets from his network. He doesn't deviate from his area of expertise, ever. He never needs a full comparative market analysis when going on a listing presentation, because he is a walking database of information: He knows his market inside and out.

He has the power because he has earned it, and no one can match him. All of his marketing, direct mail, advertising, promotional pieces and sponsored events position him as the Condo

King. This requires planning and selectivity in his direct mail and advertising.

Allan makes sure his choices maximize and reinforce his position. He is only interested in a medium or program that supports his specialized market. If it does not meet the criteria of his marketing plan and align with his strategy, he is not interested in investing the time or the money. His strategy and investment have paid off, and for his particular area, the customer comes to him! Now, that is specialization at its best!

Step #2: What's Your Niche?

It is human nature to go toward pleasure and away from pain. The same applies to how we approach life and our business. We tend to have more interest and enthusiasm for those things we like to do, and we find incredible methods of procrastination for those chores that are not our favorites.

Stop. You have identified a geographic or property type specialty. Now take a minute to assess the strong points of your career and the areas of the business that you truly enjoy. Are you the best at helping that first-time buyer, or are the small investors your passion? Next, look at your history (if you have one) and notice where your business has the largest percentage of successful transactions. Do you speak a second language? Do you enjoy working with the transferring corporate family?

Your specialization may be relieving the "transferee trauma" of moving family from one area of the country to another. Are you more comfortable with certain personality types, styles of homes, income brackets, age groups?

Once you identify a group, segmenting it even further can be fun and very profitable. The average consumer is being conditioned to service in highly specialized areas of the market. Think about it: The masses are even particular about how they want their fast-food hamburgers prepared ... fried versus broiled!

If McDonald's and Burger King can segment their marketplace, you can't afford not to. Just as you wouldn't choose a foot doctor to diagnose your heart condition, your consumer may demand a specialist. Better you than your competition!

When planning your network strategy, decide on an area of expertise. The second step takes specialization a bit further by identifying a particular niche of your market segment. By targeting a specific niche of the market and combining it with an in-depth knowledge of the subject matter, you have created a powerful, unique and distinctive position in the market you wish to penetrate.

Step #3: Combining Your Specialty with a Personal Interest

Imagine how much more fun and rewarding your career would be if you could combine a hobby or an interest with an area of expertise that offers a unique benefit to your consumer, while you have a great time earning a living. Hobbs/Herder Advertising of Santa Ana, California, has a great example of a gentleman who wanted to use niche marketing to build a network in his personal interest, fly fishing. Let's call him Fred.

Fred knew his marketing plan would need to be consistent with the fly fishing message. He carefully reworked his positioning by having a new photo taken. Rather than posing in his best suit, he chose full fishing garb, complete with fishing pole, hat and waders. His business cards and note pads incorporated a fish in the artwork, and his new logo proclaimed him to be "The Fly Fisherman Specialist."

Fred's plan was to attract people who shared his interest in fly fishing (who would refer their fly-fishing-enthusiast friends). His advertising no longer reflected the head shot photo but now sported his new logo and photo. He cleverly placed these ads in fishing magazines. His direct mail pieces were redesigned to include his new theme, along with his consistent press releases.

The result: Fred attracted customers and clients who shared his interest and who referred and networked with others of the same interest. Soon he was perceived as the Fly Fisherman Specialist. He enjoyed the "instant" rapport of people who shared his joy of fishing. He planned fishing trips with past clients and customers and reaped the rewards.

Smart? You bet! Fred has a great time listing and selling. And he makes lots of money. The specialization allowed our fisherman to create a high profile in a segment of the buying and selling market, which made his networking targeted and very effective. There are hundreds of places and groups from which to build an area of specialization. *You* get to decide your own personal direction. Of course, this does not preclude working with other customers or clients. Instead, it provides a solid base for a strong, loyal customer clientele. Others who identify with your area of expertise will become part of your client base as well.

Avenues for building relationships can include networking with groups such as the following:

- Salespeople working in services ancillary to the real estate industry, such as inspectors, appraisers and attorneys
- Past buyers and sellers
- Professionals in the area: doctors, dentists, etc.
- Community: school, church, Rotary Club, Chamber of Commerce, Little League, women's groups, men's groups
- Hobby groups: wine tasting, gourmet cooking, biking, dance, archery, etc.
- Charity groups
- Fields of specialization: commercial, military, foreign language, waterfront, second homes, first homes, rural, farms, farmettes, ranches, ranchettes, condos, townhomes, apartments, co-ops, highrises, duplexes, geographic areas, age groups
- Retirees, divorced people, single parents, religious groups, income, specific companies, sports

Generally, you will find that working in an area that complements your expertise makes the investment of time and life more fun and more rewarding. Take the time to identify where you would like to profile yourself to develop more business.

Step #4: Developing Your Personal Marketing Plan

To establish an effective personal promotion and marketing campaign, you need to position yourself as a value to clients, so that they will think of you when they have a real estate need. First, you must get down to basics. We talked about developing those things that will help identify you in the pool of agents in your area. You are the one who needs to assess where you are presently and to determine what is needed to increase your business. You are the only one who can identify and implement a personal marketing plan that works for you and your marketplace. How will things change in a year's time? For your volume, business and contacts to change, you must implement new steps. This is accomplished through a personal marketing plan that includes these elements:

- An identifiable logo
- Stationery and direct mail that identify you first and then your company affiliation
- A planned direct mail program on a consistent basis that gives consumers information they want or need
- Positioning through press releases
- Print and media exposure in your advertising and in magazines

By developing a common theme with your advertising, direct mail, stationery and business cards that sets you apart from your company and competition, your chances of recall improve dramatically. If you are not feeling creative, employ an advertising company to help you create the message you want to send. Remember Fred the fisherman? His agency (Hobbs/Herder, Santa Ana, California) has helped some top producers obtain market share with innovative ways to establish client/customer recall.

This common thread will tie your efforts together in all phases of your personal marketing. The farm specialist will possibly consider placing ads in rural newspapers rather than in the *Wall Street*

Journal or *Crain's Chicago Business*. The transferee specialist will network with other specializers in neighboring boards to cover the gaps in corporate relocation.

Step #5: Developing Promotional Materials for Your Target Market

People need to identify you, the person, first, and then your company affiliation, so a photo is imperative. If you are adamant about skipping the photo part, find an artist to do a memorable logo sketch. With any promotional piece, be sure to check with your management for approval to be sure your message is harmonious with the company's philosophy. If possible, reflect the theme of your service in the photo.

Consider the following ways to present yourself:

- If new construction is your niche, consider having a photo taken with an unfinished house being built in the background and a couple of rolls of blueprints under your arm.
- Thinking of specializing in retirement housing? A photo in a business suit won't send a consistent message.
- Rural farms your specialty? The suit won't work here either. Get your overalls out! Help people remember and connect with you by giving them a visual aid.

Finally, whatever you are direct mailing, be sure that you have adhered to all the guidelines for both your company and the profession to avoid problems later. Have a consistent look for the mailing program, as well as your press releases and other media contributions. Consistency will be a key foundation for establishing client/customer recall.

Step #6: Implementing a Long-Term Strategy for Customer Contacts

People love being remembered, because it makes them feel important. Keeping in touch long after the business transaction is completed helps alleviate the abandoned feeling many customers have after the sale. Design a regular personal means of keeping in contact. Sending out birthday cards is one way; there are many other ways of building clients for life.

Step #7: Planning Strategic Events with a Personal Touch

Hosting an annual party or event gives you several opportunities to keep the channels open (see Chapter 10, "Keeping Your Clients for Life"). You get the opportunity to invite, check up on an RSVP, send an invitation, send a follow-up thank you with a photo or two and see each other face to face in a neutral, positive and fun environment. This is a great time to find out if they or their friends need your services.

Barbecues, picnics, holiday theme parties, sports events, local events and local functions all provide opportunities to meet with people who can bring you more business, in a warm and giving situation.

Step #8: Getting "Techy"

If you have silently decided that you are going to keep track of business the way you usually do, you won't have to worry about it for too long. The information highway is growing so fast that it will be more difficult the longer you wait. It will be necessary to be online with your listings and office management. Programs like SuperStar Computing (Eden Prairie, Minnesota) make both the selection of hardware and the training and support one-stop shopping. The consumer will have as much as or more information than you do and will be more sophisticated about getting it. This isn't a choice; it's a matter of *when*, or you definitely will be out of the business.

If you're not interested in technology at this reading, spend some money on something you can't wear—a computer! Gone are the days of 3" X 5" cards in a file. This is the age of information, and you need to be there too. You are probably not working dollar-productively if you are not using a computer to minimize your mailings, labeling and information files. The good news is that it is getting easier and cheaper.

Don't miss this step or you will be out of the loop of the technology age and out of the loop with your clients and customers. If you are out of the loop, don't be surprised to see a competitor in your place.

Step #9: Tracking the Referrals

One thing you can be sure of is that people enjoy being thanked for their efforts. Always say thank you immediately when someone refers a client or a customer to you. Do it with flowers, candy, cookies, bouquets, gift baskets ... do something now! Sending a personalized coffee mug and filling it with a fun and personal gift says thank you over and over again. I personally like to send what I call "coffee breaks." This gift includes my personalized coffee mug and a gourmet coffee or chocolate.

It's not enough to say thank you that one time. Keep a list of contacts who continually refer you business, and keep them in mind to thank again, possibly at Thanksgiving. People love being remembered for the good things they have done over the year, and you want them to know that you are still very grateful to them. Here's when that logo and slogan come back for double duty. Always say thank you on one of your own note cards—it pays!

Step #10: Using Personal Marketing in Your Prelisting Packet

Want more listings? According to NAR statistics, less than 4 percent of agents have a personal marketing piece or brochure that identifies them in the sea of more than 700,000 licensed agents. That means if a seller is interviewing three agents to list his or her home, chances are two of them have no positioning piece to separate their personal identity from that of their company. What's wrong with that, you ask? The seller most likely will never meet Mr. Coldwell or Mr. Century! You are the person they are looking to hire to market their home, so they need to know why they should employ *you* over the others.

This can be done easily and elegantly by using a prelisting or preconfirmation packet before the seller ever meets you for the appointment. "Priming the pump" saves you from having to convince the seller what a terrific salesperson you are. The testimonial method is much less arrogant and more easily accepted.

This can be accomplished by skillfully assembling a packet of information that the homeowner can review prior to actually meeting you. This packet *must* contain information and positioning pieces primarily on you and your accomplishments, and secondarily some information about the company. This prelisting packet is delivered by courier or overnight delivery to your prospective client for his or her perusal and study. (It's delivered to you, the reader, in Appendix A.)

The letter you include confirms your appointment time and date and asks the seller to complete a "homework" sheet, enclosed to make the appointment time more efficient. This puts you, the agent, in control.

The homework sheet requests that the seller have ready several documents for his or her property, along with a set of keys and other information, all of which sends this message: "I am a professional. My time is valuable. Please have these items available for the time we spend discussing the marketing of your home."

A seller is then put on notice: "This agent has his or her act together. Unlike other agents who just had promotional information on their company, this person is asking me to prepare for this appointment, so who is interviewing whom?" It definitely puts the seller on notice that you are on target to get the job done!

Other items to include in your prelisting packet are:

- Your personal mission statement
- A list of *B* team services to aid the seller in getting the home in marketable condition

- If an attorney is used for closings in your area, a list of attorneys for the seller's consideration
- A list of questions for the seller to ask prospective agents that will help him or her determine the agent to use. Superstar Walter Sanford has a list of 20 questions I have adopted and included in Appendix A to give you an idea of how to direct the homeowner to appreciate your expertise.
- A "communication direction." This report tells the seller what to expect in the first four weeks of your marketing time.
- Your personal bio, including awards, designations, committee appointments, etc.
- A "just so you know how we work" report. This communication lets the seller know how you handle the different aspects of the marketing and processing of his or her listing. It is imperative that the seller actually sign this report so there are no miscommunications later. When you make your objectives clear and clarify several points, the expectations of sellers are clearer.
- Testimonials from satisfied past clients and customers. You can include copies of three or four letters from happy homeowners and buyers that sing your praises. Some top agents include a list of people with phone numbers and addresses for prospective homeowners to contact. (Be sure to get permission first!)
- Your company promotional material, along with samples of direct mail pieces, copies of recent ads from magazines and newspapers, promotional articles on you that have been reprinted, etc.

As a matter of course, include highlights of the kinds of special and customized marketing you have used, but do not include a full marketing plan unless the homeowner is willing to list with you. Why give the competition an edge on how you work?

This information kit presells *you* before you get there and fits well into a personalized or company folder sporting your business card with photo and logo. By selling your expertise before you actually meet the homeowners, you increase your chances of making a great professional first impression!

Even More Ideas for You To Try

Salesperson-to-Salesperson Contact

I recently received a buyer referral from a competitor company located in the next town. A woman had called from out of state requesting an appointment to see a particular price and style of home on her upcoming trip to our area. The broker referred me (over his own franchise company located in my town) to handle her special need, as I handle more of what she wanted in my area.

When I received her call, I was quite surprised that she found me. I immediately called the referring broker, thanked him sincerely and sent a confirming letter to pay a fee should her meeting result in a sale. One phone call and follow-up letter have generated thousands of dollars for yours truly.

That scenario is the payoff of my networking strategy: board interaction, referring customers to the other agent's appraisal business and general respect for his office and position in our board.

Ancillary Relationships Pay!

Ancillary and me: A man was flying back to Chicago from Florida. He began a conversation with a woman, whose name he later could not remember, discussing his disappointment with his real estate service. He did, however, remember my name when she spoke highly of my professionalism, service level and energy. When I found out about the conversation, it took me awhile to figure out who was kind enough to remember me.

Interestingly, the woman was an appraiser for a firm I had done work with in the past. Early in her career and still a little unfamiliar with our area, she called several times a day for floor plans, information on past sales, square footage and with other questions. We patiently helped her through many appraisals. Now she is living out of our area but still returning the favor. The power of networking lives on.

Building the Power of the Network

For my networking strategy, I find it is imperative to give any kind of support and information to the appraisers when they call. Try to have all the documentation and information ready to help them do their job. The relationship base built here can help later when you have a question or need their opinion so you can be more accurate when rendering a professional opinion.

It is prudent to keep a list of several attorneys to whom you can refer clients. When I do refer a client to a lawyer, I make sure that the counselor knows the client was referred by me. Several great leads have been the result of a good working relationship with an attorney and the attorney's support staff.

At the holidays, think about a small gift for the support staff. It lets them know how very much you appreciate their good service and patient cooperation during the year. They will remember you when a business opportunity presents itself. Never underestimate the power of staff. They can make or break you with their support—or lack of it.

Don't overlook loan officers and lenders in your area. Oftentimes, they are aware of families trading up to a larger home or investigating new purchase power for a possible transfer. As a lender often occupies a position of confidence and trust, giving yours can be quite profitable!

Past buyers and sellers are a fantastic resource for networking. It takes more than a gift at closing to nurture the relationship, however. Even if they had a positive transaction with you, the ability to remember fades unless you choose to nurture the relationship. Positioning yourself so they hear from you once a month will guarantee that you are remembered.

With the initial needs fulfilled, you might consider personalizing your approach: gifts, notes, birthday cards and neighborhood information they would have an interest in. As clients and customers are often in a position to recommend your services, be sure they remember you as helpful and caring. The last thing you want is for them to forget you because you pestered them with generic, impersonal real estate junk. Most real estate agents do.

The attitude in networking has to be "do what you can to promote the business of the other person," and he or she will want to return the favor. The motivation here is to sincerely and genuinely promote their expertise because you respect and admire their service level and professional integrity.

Use the Power of Affiliate Memberships To Build Networking

Let's presume you are a member of several of the affiliate organizations in our profession, like the Women's Council of REALTORS® and the National Association of REALTORS® Residential Sales Council. Profiling yourself within and with the affiliate groups depends on the amount of time you are willing to devote at state and national meetings and the level of your involvement.

Many of my personal referrals come from these state and national affiliations. I get several calls a month from salespeople in other parts of the country choosing me over their own franchise affiliate because of my alliance with the group. Attending state and national meetings builds friendships and recognition that just keeps growing. Both councils have printed nationwide rosters that offer the name of a professional in almost every corner of the country for easy and dependable referral contacts.

Work Those Conventions!

After returning from a state or national meeting, I take a stack of business cards I have collected and mail a short note on stationery with my photo saying, "It was great meeting you at the recent meetings. Please keep me in mind if you have someone coming to our area." Enclose a list of the towns and areas you cover.

I recommend this personal touch over a simple card exchange at a convention. Chances are they will arrive home with their own stack of cards and file them where there will be little or no recall. Profiling yourself with a little extra touch guarantees their attention when they are comfortably back in their office and filing you in the proper spot.

Enlist Local Support

If you have been in the real estate business for any length of time, you may have seen this situation: A listing is about to expire, and the client definitely wants exposure and the services of another real estate company. Offer to pay a referral to those agents who will refer you their about-to-expire listings. You get the listing, they get a healthy referral fee and the seller gets sold.

This is a win-win proposition for everybody involved. Rather than lose the entire investment of the original listing period, when time and money were spent trying to get a property sold, you can help everybody make money and defer your losses!

Community Strategy: The Person First, the REALTOR® Second

Opportunities abound in the town and county in which you live. You need only to decide what areas to interface with. Church group work is the favorite of some professionals. Some of our most successful agents pour plenty of hours into church support activities.

Don't be a "secret" agent. Although it's imperative that you profile as a real person first, it's helpful that you let people know you make your living as a real estate professional. By interacting on a personal level first, it is often easier for members of the church to approach you on your business side with confidence.

Does your town or community have parades or charity benefits? This is a perfect time to gain visibility. Showing that you are interested in improving or promoting your town enhances you both personally and professionally. Getting involved with supporting local groups is an excellent way to establish local relationships. You might even make new friends and have a great time.

When it comes to community involvement, people like to work with people who also care about their community—you!

Go for It!

Networking reaps rewards from virtually every facet of our business. You can expand your professional dimension by using the continuous flow of previously unsolicited opportunities. Beware of botching a referral—you are only as good as your last referral.

Bad news travels incredibly fast and can negatively position the person who made the referral or other contact. Don't be afraid to say no, or refer to another, if time or personal problems limit your ability to provide service.

A final word here. Contribute to your profession through your integrity, practice of fair ethics and guidance without always expecting immediate gratification. You can contribute by sharing your talents and expertise in a small way, like training at your board, or in a larger way, by sharing your thoughts in articles or briefs. It's not so much what you do or even how you contribute; what's critical is that you do it!

Chapter 10

Keeping Your Clients for Life

*A*n old Girl Scout song says: "Make new friends, but keep the old; one is silver and the other is gold." I believe this venerable song's message should be the basis, and at the very heart, of every real estate agent's operations. Repeat and referral business is totally dependent upon this type of career-building philosophy. It's a shame so many agents miss out on the golden opportunities that can arise when you maintain contact with past clients. Many will do the far more difficult work of cold-prospecting for new business—a necessity, to be sure—but they do so at the expense of keeping in touch with past clients. Keeping warm referrals alive is not only more pleasant, it is much more profitable, and that's an unbeatable combination.

Finding Effective Ways of Keeping in Touch

Your past clients have (or should have) established common ground with you. Their attitude toward you is warm and friendly and their interest in you is genuine. After all, you helped solve a very big problem or need they had. Your subsequent contacts are nonthreatening because you are not selling or trying to influence them in any way, at least not perceptibly. If you have done a good job for them, they will think of you every time real estate comes up in their conversations. If you don't capitalize on this favorable predisposition, you're making a serious mistake.

Many agents say, "I'm embarrassed. I haven't spoken to them since the closing." If, in the qualifying stages and during your numerous presale contacts, you were keeping accurate notes, this should present no problem for you. Dig into your file (which should be retained as standard procedure) and you'll find plenty of things to refer to or discuss—birthdays, anniversaries, children and special interests or hobbies. You already have this information, so make it work for you a second or third time, maybe more. Because of the nature of the information, you're automatically on a personal, nonselling level, so recontacts will be easy. Even a simple phone call just to touch base can be the key to re-establishing the relationship.

Here are some simple guidelines to follow to help you contact past clients and customers with elegance and professionalism to ensure they enjoy hearing from you.

1. Establish a direct mail program with an identifiable theme in colors used, logo, slogan and photo for maximum recognition.
2. Set up a program of contacts at regular intervals. Make it an efficient, ongoing service.
3. Concentrate on being personal in your approach and try to be unique.

Without a plan for follow-up, you can expect only modest results, if any. It is really like throwing money out the window. I would bet that when sitting at the closing table, I have just acquired a new past customer—the one that the other agent has worked some 60-plus hours to attain, and most likely will abandon after the sale. Chances are better than 90 percent that the family across the table will be contacted less than once a year, if at all. A recent issue of *US News and World Report* contained a survey that revealed the biggest reason for loss of business was that 68 percent of the salespeople had an attitude of indifference toward their customers.

Set Up a Monthly Call Program

Each and every month (or weekly), without fail, call five or six past clients just to let them know you're thinking of them. Perhaps they've painted their new home or landscaped their grounds; if so, you could call to say how much you like what they did. Or perhaps something you know about their prior home might interest them. Old memories do linger.

Get Personal!

Update Information

Check out the "People and Promotions" section of your newspaper for career promotions and other such information. People love the recognition and are impressed that you took the time to send a personal note. Notify your past clients of new listings and of property sold (especially if homes are comparable). A "For Your Information" note will be appreciated and certainly lets your past clients know you are thinking of them. This is a great way to subtly accent your professionalism and let it be known that you are on top of things. If their friends like your past client's new home and neighborhood, your information about a new listing should be put to good use (with you the beneficiary).

Check the Local Newspaper

Clip any notices about your clients (trips they've taken, Little League or school awards and the like) and send them a card or note along with the clipping. This personal attention is really appreciated and not soon forgotten.

Send Inexpensive Gifts

There are numerous small but useful household items that you can send periodically. The key here is the usefulness, not the expense. These reminders, of course, should carry your name to be really effective, as well as your phone number. Be sure that your choice of gifts carries the theme of your logo, slogan and your personal marketing strategy. If you had a quarterly gift program, surely a calendar would be one idea you might want to consider.

Happy Birthdays Make You a Happy Agent!

The technical side of our world makes us more efficient but less personal. The warmth of person-to-person will most always be paramount to a cold and impersonal corporate contact. Birthdays are the one day each of us feels special in some way. It marks a day that is really all our own. In our busy world, too few of our friends and family take the time to send a birthday greeting. People all want the same things in life—recognition, appreciation, love.

A great way to keep personal contact is to send birthday cards to your sphere of influence. This is particularly effective with past clients. It's an easy habit to get into. When you have your initial interview, take a 3" x 5" card and list the days and the months of the household birthdays. You may even want to include the pets! Transfer to a simple January–December file box and write out all the cards for the month in advance. Getting your own signature cards printed with your special logo lets the birthday person know the greeting comes from you, not the company.

The card can simply say:

Hi!
Just thinking about you on your special day. Have a great one!
Hugs....
Terri Murphy

Be sure to include a business card, so they have your phone number handy. If the card is for a child, enclose some McDonald's gift certificates for fun. The envelope should be plain (no company stuff here!) and hand-written. Also, include fun stickers both outside and in! We get great response years and years later from people who know we still care about them. It is a real delight when a past client who now lives 1,000 miles away sends a return note saying he or she was thrilled to hear from you!

Go Public!

Holiday Contact for the Smart Agent

When the herd is going in one direction, that is your clue to go the other way. Everybody sends the predictable Christmas and New Year's holiday card. I prefer to spend my time and money where it will get the most attention. A great example is Super Bowl Sunday. How many clients and customers expect a gift or card on this day? I send a can of popcorn with the teams' names on it to all the people who referred business to me during the year. I find this generates a lot more attention than a holiday greeting. By the end of January, people are ready for a little surprise and the gesture really stands out. Send your personal note card to ensure the recipient knows the gift came from you and not your company (complete with your photo, of course) with a note that says: "Thanks for the referrals. I love having you on my team!"

You can select any secondary holiday and capitalize on it. Halloween, Valentine's Day and May Day, for instance, are holidays you can use in promotional campaigns. Send cards with appropriate decals on the envelope for attention-getting purposes (small children love the colorful art). A business card magnet or one for the refrigerator is very appropriate. Another alternative is an inexpensive gift tied to the occasion or the event you've "promoted." This attention will go a long way.

Have an Annual Party!

Beth Mason-Massey, superstar from Virginia, has held an annual Pig Pickin' party for over ten years now. The event features brightly colored plastic cups embellished with pig designs. When each guest arrives, a hostess writes the guest's name on a cup. Every year each guest gets a personalized cup of a different color to keep as a memento.

Beth hires a band or a DJ for musical entertainment, roasts about 300 pounds of pork and invites more than 600 past clients, customers, friends and affiliates. Generally, about 300 make it to the event, rain or shine. A press release, complete with photos, is sent to her local newspaper.

Beth gets great mileage from this occasion by

- sending a fun invitation (contact #1),
- asking for an RSVP (contact #2),
- seeing the person at the event (contact #3),
- giving a personalized cup (contact #4) and
- sending a note along with a picture taken with her at the party (contact #5).

Five contacts for one event. That's not bad. And it must work. Beth continues to be among the top ten producers for her company, Long & Foster.

At parties of this sort, few expect fancy gourmet meals. They should, in fact, be informal affairs. If you decide to throw such a party, you'll find you have a number of volunteer cooks in your midst. Men especially love to show their outdoor cooking skills.

Don't Forget Special Community Events

If, for example, your local women's club or some other civic group is sponsoring an event, purchase a few extra tickets and invite your most recently transferred clients. This is a perfect way for them to make new acquaintances—something they may be having difficulty doing on their own—and your thoughtfulness will be greatly appreciated. This is a perfect example of a personal gift, yet your investment will be as modest as it is meaningful.

Keep at It!

There are many other ways to keep in touch with your clients and prospects. The ideas below have been tried successfully by some of the industry superstars. One or more of them may fit into your overall plan for keeping in touch with your clients and prospects.

1. Send a newspaper clipping or an informative article that centers around the career or hobby of a past client or a present prospect.
2. Participate in a local charity drive.
3. Participate in a food pantry drive or other worthwhile community event.
4. Initiate holiday cookie exchanges in your farm neighborhood.
5. Organize a block party.
6. Publish a neighborhood directory.
7. Establish a local networking chapter breakfast meeting.
8. Provide finance/refinance information.
9. Send the latest tax information to past clients.

Superstars' Secrets for Follow-up

After interviewing and brainstorming with some of the top industry leaders, I've learned that the contacts are made from four to 12 times a year, depending on the market. The key here is to be able to contact your clients in a personal and attentive way, while positioning yourself as their REALTOR® for life. The client or customer will always be receptive to information that pertains to some level of personal interest. It's like buying a piano. If you are not in the market to buy a piano, your interest in the sales flyer is only minimal. The same applies to your past clients. Give them the "personal touch," not information that they may not need or want.

Walter Sanford of Long Beach, California, has been one of the most innovative agents in nurturing past clients. Walter starts early, using the talents of his *B* team to establish a cohesive synergy of service that continues long after the closing. When Walter does a listing presentation, his mortgage and title companies, home inspectors and others all send letters to the prospective client selling the Sanford full-service team.

After the property has sold, Walter supplies the seller with postcards he or she can use to notify friends and family of his or her new address. Of course, Walter's photo is on the card, and his team will cheerfully save the clients the work and mail the cards for them. This opens the door to "warm" call the seller's sphere of influence and reinforce the exceptional service of the Sanford team, in a friendly, value-added-service way. It also provides the opportunity for Walter to ask for interested parties who might be listing or selling in the future.

Phil Herman, superstar from Dayton, Ohio, has a plan that is so strong he retains virtually all of his past clientele. Phil calls his clients the day after closing to make sure everything is satisfactory in the home. He follows up one week after the closing to confirm that there are no latent problems and to be certain the family has settled into their new surroundings. The same family will be contacted 30 days from closing to verify that they have received any paperwork that had to be forwarded to them. The next follow-up call occurs 60 days later with a similar "touch base" contact. The next call, which is placed six months later, is a friendly "just checking" call.

Through Phil's great system, the customer or client, now technically a new customer, is contacted on a regular basis four to six times per year. This family is undoubtedly impressed with the personal care and attention Phil gives. How many of us have just abandoned the family after handing them a plant or a basket of flowers after the closing?

Closing gifts may be a nice touch in the right circumstances. Personally, I feel that my professional service is the gift, and only in some cases do I feel that something extra is necessary. I didn't receive a gift from my attorney, accountant or doctor the last time I used their services, and I feel I offer my clients the same level of professionalism. The client/customer will be very impressed with the care and attention you provide. It works for Phil. The fact that he sells more than 100 homes per year will attest to that!

There are so many ways you can keep the channels of communication open with past clients. I could offer many other suggestions, and so can you if you put your mind to it—and you should!

Follow-up helps ensure that you won't drive by one day and see a competitor's sign in *your* listing's front yard. If you haven't contacted your client or customer, you shouldn't expect loyalty.

The important thing to remember is that a past client is a most valuable resource—one you worked diligently for and, in a real sense, earned. If you do not legitimately and professionally capitalize on this, you are doing yourself a real disservice. Put your creativity to work and harness this resource. Yes, continue to make new friends, but certainly keep the old ones.

Epilogue

*I*t's been a long road down MLS Lane for me over the past 17-plus years. Thankfully, I learned from my mistakes when to head in another direction. The old Monday morning quarterback routine comes into play—if I only knew then what I know now.

Real estate is not at all like retail, where you get to lock the doors at 5 PM and walk away. It's a people business, and with people, things happen when they happen, not necessarily before 5 o'clock! Real estate will control you unless you take control.

I learned this lesson the hard way. It took a major trauma to get my face out of the MLS book and examine my priorities. You can get carried away with the service and the follow-up and the direct mail and the networking. Although I have no regrets, I can look back from here and see where I passed up a lot of life in between, from being desperate, too scared or just plain working too much.

Know that success and new learning skills are compounding elements that we build on every day. Start early with the full calendar of your year and block out the times for "real" life—you know, the vacation with the family, your workout days, your veg days, your designation seminar days (GRI, CRS, LTG, etc.), your personal days (hair, doctors, dentists, etc.)—and then fill in the rest with the designated workdays. Yes, designated. I know that people write offers at any time, and it's usually on the day your sister is getting married and you are in the wedding party.

Life will go on in spite of real estate, so we need to keep this business in perspective. Although I respect the urgency of presenting offers and taking listings, I also respect the need to give yourself and your life priority. Generally, those houses will be there in the morning and you can conduct business in somewhat reasonable hours. Make this your personal call to do what is appropriate for you. I found myself dropping whatever I was doing *at that moment* to run to present an offer or list a house and be of service. I am suggesting that you can actually finish your dinner or wait until your son's soccer game is over to do the real estate tasks, and everyone will still survive.

Watch Your Word-Crafting!

You might be wondering what I am referring to when I say *word-crafting*. You know, that chatter going on in your head most of the time is potent stuff. That is where we can literally talk ourselves into success, depression, happiness, sadness, health and illness. I live by the words "You name it, you claim it and you get it." You create your own reality by what you think about and say to yourself on a daily basis. How many times have you heard yourself say, "It's just not like me to do over $5 million a year," or "I just can't lose this ten pounds"?

Look around your life objectively and take full responsibility for where you are, what you are, what you have or don't have. You might see a pattern in what you "believe" about yourself. Instead of believing all the negative things you hear, just for today, believe all the outrageously wonderful ideas you hear. What a difference that could make in how we feel about ourselves and how we view our world. There are enough negative thinkers around. Choose to think good things about yourself and others. It will make your life a much more pleasant place to live.

Include Those Daily "10s" in Your Life

Do you remember when we talked about Dr. Fred Grosse back in Chapter 3? Dr. Grosse teaches us how to fill our days with what he calls "number 10s," which are wonderful, nurturing experiences. Lacing our day with "10" experiences helps us to feel fulfilled and keeps us focused on productively handling our daily activities.

A cup of morning coffee becomes a real "10" when we enjoy a gourmet cappuccino with a good friend. The same coffee experience could be a "100" if it were on the French Riviera with the love of your life. Know that sooner and hopefully not later, you will learn that it is the journey that is exciting; there are no destinations, just crossroads.

I wouldn't be truthful if I didn't share with you that this real estate world can be tough and sometimes relentless. Incorporate those little celebrations during the moments of your day, to pamper yourself. It can be anything from a piece of music to a single flower on your desk just for you. Don't wait for someone else to indulge you. *You* indulge you. Making the road interesting, colorful and as nurturing as possible will help you feel so much more productive, vital and pleasant to be with. There will always be more business, another listing, another offer to present. Accent the moments of your life with those things that pass your way only once. It's okay—take a break; just know what can change you and make you feel nurtured, loved and centered again.

If You Break Your Body, Where Will You Live?

Take care of yourself. Remember Rule #1 on My List in Chapter 4? Always leave time for #1! When I think of what we take for granted in life, our health often tops the list. Although there are no marathons for the real estate industry, being in good physical, mental and emotional shape is a prerequisite. It's the easiest career in which to cheat on yourself and become the ultimate loser.

To avoid that fate, make appointments to sit down and eat a lunch that brings health instead of robbing you of it. Schedule some form of physical activity that will make you feel good. Without fail, focus on giving yourself a specified time for quiet, time for creativity, time just for you. Take the mental break to see where you are headed, what you've learned from where you have been and how to produce different results. Start now. Start today, even for ten minutes. It will regenerate the spirit. Take care of yourself. We need you!

Believe in the Power of Compounding

Whether it is ten minutes a day for exercising or $10 a week of savings, over a period of years you've got some accumulation. In the positive sense this is a very powerful thought process. Think about how it relates to so many phases of our lives. Farming regularly every week for 52 weeks a year times three years equals 156 weeks of farming and guaranteed name recognition! Walking one mile a day every day for a year equals 365 miles! Now, multiply that by a lifetime. There is awesome power in compounding that can work either negatively or positively.

You choose. Start investing in yourself this moment. Begin by giving yourself 15 minutes a day to take a walk with the dog, or with your significant other, or with a friend. Know that even one negative thought can compound into talking yourself right out of some of the best things in life. Start putting away that 20 percent of your income today and learn to live on the rest. The reverse is tragic. Pay yourself first and avoid being a "bag lady" when you retire ... unless the bag is a Gucci! Tell the people you are close to how much they mean to you and how much you love them, today, while you can and as often as you can. Use the positive powers of compounding as a tool for building a rich and successful life.

The Power of Commitment

This is my favorite. How many times does someone make a promise to do something for you and it just never happens? The speaker's intentions are probably from the heart, but somewhere the action gets lost. Think how your sense of integrity can develop if your word means something. Following up on a promise makes the other person feel great, and you get to feel even greater. Not just because you followed through, but because your personal integrity grows and you get to feel good about yourself. Do yourself a favor, and don't say it if you can't do it. Don't promise if you can't deliver. The best solution is to underpromise and overdeliver. This dazzles the recipient and you become the hero.

Practice this in every phase of your life. Harmony on the inside feels so much better than another thought of unfinished business that hangs around like clutter in your heart and head. Make the choice that your word is 24-karat gold and given not foolishly or lightly but with solid thought, power and an action plan. Your kids will love it and learn from it. Your clients and customers will brag about you, and your loved ones will feel cherished and important, as well they should.

The Power of Saying Thank You

Sometimes these words can't mean enough, and sometimes they are said and mean so little. All of us want the same things in life. We want the feeling of being appreciated. This is one of the biggies. In our business, success is always a team effort. You can't make the sale without the help of lots of people. The closing happens as a result of the actions of many to accomplish the transfer. Take every opportunity to say thank you to all who have worked in the background to make you a success. That would be your *B* team. Find ways that go beyond just a thank-you note, although this is a fine gesture.

Think about sending "thank you" coffee breaks as gifts. Thank the title company representative who helped at a tough closing. Thank the attorney's secretary. Thank the lender. Thank the other agent for helping you sell. Thank the person who referred you business immediately with flowers or a coffee break gift. When you wake up in the morning, thank your significant other for sharing life with you again this day. However you choose to say these magical words, make sure the beneficiary knows that you mean it. The power of the well-meant thank you is magnificent!

Get Good Fixes

Not every day starts out a great day in real estate. W. Mitchell, treasured friend and author of *The Man Who Would Not Be Defeated*, tells us it is not what happens to us, it's what we do about it. Read about people who have faced challenges that go way beyond losing a listing, a buyer or whatever you may be moping about at the moment. It will put things back in perspective for you.

Arm yourself with a select group of friends who will help you get back on track. Start or find a group that meets by phone at least once a month to exchange new ideas, new techniques, strategies and war stories that can invigorate and energize you. Your local competition may be thrilled that you are experiencing a challenge or having a bad day, so working outside the local realm may feel safer and provide a new perspective. There are mastermind groups forming everywhere. Be sure to choose a group in which the people involved are doing more business than you, so you can learn from them. Align yourself with the winners who can show you new ways to win.

Over 33 Flavors To Choose From

Some of the ideas we have shared here may work just great for you and others won't quite seem to fit. That's perfectly all right. The best part of life is that there are lots of flavors and combinations to choose from to make it interesting and exciting. Some work better than others. Check them all out and see what fits you. As you travel the road, you'll come across plenty of crazy ideas, some of which are appropriate for your way of doing business and are consistent with your mission plan; others simply won't do. Make the choices that are right for you and don't worry about the critics, as you can always count on them to be there.

My favorite quote is from President Theodore Roosevelt on the subject of critics:

It is not the critic that counts, nor the man who points out where the strong man stumbled or where the doer of deeds could have done them better. The credit belongs to the man who is actually in the arena, whose face is marred with dust and sweat and blood. At best, he knows the triumph of high achievement; if he fails, at least he fails while daring greatly, so that his place shall never be with those cold and timid souls who knew neither victory nor defeat.

From My Heart to Yours

I guess if someone had told me how tough (or how terrific) real estate would be for me all those years ago, I may not have taken the first step. As you may have surmised, I have been blessed with an abundance of good friends, guidance, learning experiences and challenges that chiseled new dimensions in my life and career. Those of you who have small children know about those rough spots in life that you would love to keep them from having to endure. That is about how I feel about you in your journey in real estate. Hopefully, through this book, I can shortcut the harder lessons by sharing some of the things and people who have so generously helped me when I was whining and going through boot camp before earning my stripes.

The passages can be fascinating and the characters along the way amusing, thought-provoking and memorable. Enjoy the steps and do not be afraid. Know that *only you* can give the gifts of your commitment and caring to those people who seek your help and guidance. Know that the ability to earn a living will happen anyway when you are truly dedicated to helping others through your expertise.

The author Viki King writes that we must use "eternal vigilance" in our pursuit and focus in our lives. Get into curiosity instead of judgment about everything, including real estate. Choose to use the experiences and challenges your life provides to weave a rich and ornate tapestry. Embellish it with the interesting lessons and opportunities you have been blessed with. See every challenge and failure as another means of polishing you, the diamond, to a brilliance and a luster that is unmatchable by anyone or anything. Work harder on yourself than you do on your job. Keep your power and create your life the way you want. Let real estate pave the way to extraordinary personal growth and financial success.

Ciao!

The Ultimate
Prelisting Package

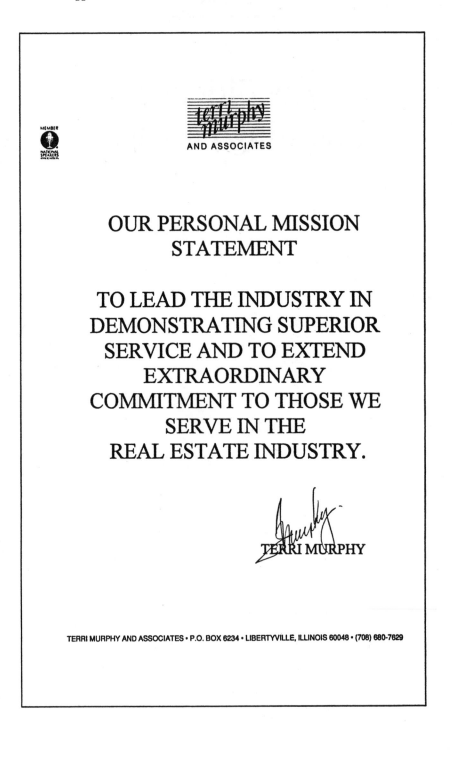

MEMBER
NATIONAL SPEAKERS ASSOCIATION

AND ASSOCIATES

OUR PERSONAL MISSION STATEMENT

TO LEAD THE INDUSTRY IN DEMONSTRATING SUPERIOR SERVICE AND TO EXTEND EXTRAORDINARY COMMITMENT TO THOSE WE SERVE IN THE REAL ESTATE INDUSTRY.

TERRI MURPHY

TERRI MURPHY AND ASSOCIATES • P.O. BOX 6234 • LIBERTYVILLE, ILLINOIS 60048 • (708) 680-7629

AND ASSOCIATES

ASK ABOUT OUR SPECIAL MARKETING PLAN

TO SELL YOUR HOME!

INCLUDING:

* TARGETED DIRECT MARKETING SERVICES THROUGH DIRECT MARKETING SERVICES OF LAKE FOREST

* TELEMARKETING WARM LEADS THRU KGS TELEMARKETING SERVICES

* VIDEO BROCHURES THROUGH DAVE ALLEN PRODUCTIONS FOR EXPOSURE TO TRANSFEREE BUYERS AND RELOCATION/THIRD PARTY COMPANIES

* REALTY VISION TELEVISION EXPOSURE

* THE HOME TOUR/ELECTRONIC ADVERTISING

* PRINT MEDIA INCLUDING: Lake County Real Estate Magazine, Harmon Homes, REMAX HOME GUIDE, The Chicago Tribune, Paddock Publications and Lakeland News-

* Insertions in Local Lakeland Papers in 4 color glossy

* Star Power National Network of top producing agents nationwide with monthly networking and mastermind sessions

* REMAX as well as CRS, and the Women's Council of Realtors for lateral marketing

Ask for our customed program designed especially for your property!

TERRI MURPHY AND ASSOCIATES • P.O. BOX 6234 • LIBERTYVILLE, ILLINOIS 60048 • (708) 680-7629

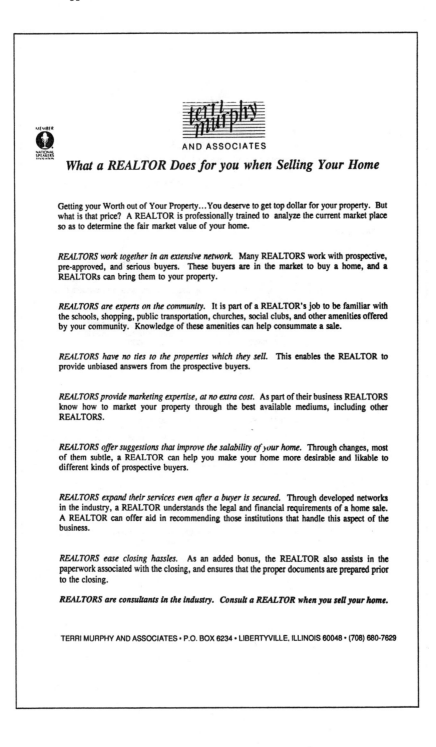

MEMBER

NATIONAL
SPEAKERS
ASSOCIATION

AND ASSOCIATES

What a REALTOR Does for you when Selling Your Home

Getting your Worth out of Your Property...You deserve to get top dollar for your property. But what is that price? A REALTOR is professionally trained to analyze the current market place so as to determine the fair market value of your home.

REALTORS work together in an extensive network. Many REALTORS work with prospective, pre-approved, and serious buyers. These buyers are in the market to buy a home, and a REALTORs can bring them to your property.

REALTORS are experts on the community. It is part of a REALTOR's job to be familiar with the schools, shopping, public transportation, churches, social clubs, and other amenities offered by your community. Knowledge of these amenities can help consummate a sale.

REALTORS have no ties to the properties which they sell. This enables the REALTOR to provide unbiased answers from the prospective buyers.

REALTORS provide marketing expertise, at no extra cost. As part of their business REALTORS know how to market your property through the best available mediums, including other REALTORS.

REALTORS offer suggestions that improve the salability of your home. Through changes, most of them subtle, a REALTOR can help you make your home more desirable and likable to different kinds of prospective buyers.

REALTORS expand their services even after a buyer is secured. Through developed networks in the industry, a REALTOR understands the legal and financial requirements of a home sale. A REALTOR can offer aid in recommending those institutions that handle this aspect of the business.

REALTORS ease closing hassles. As an added bonus, the REALTOR also assists in the paperwork associated with the closing, and ensures that the proper documents are prepared prior to the closing.

REALTORS are consultants in the industry. Consult a REALTOR when you sell your home.

TERRI MURPHY AND ASSOCIATES • P.O. BOX 6234 • LIBERTYVILLE, ILLINOIS 60048 • (708) 680-7629

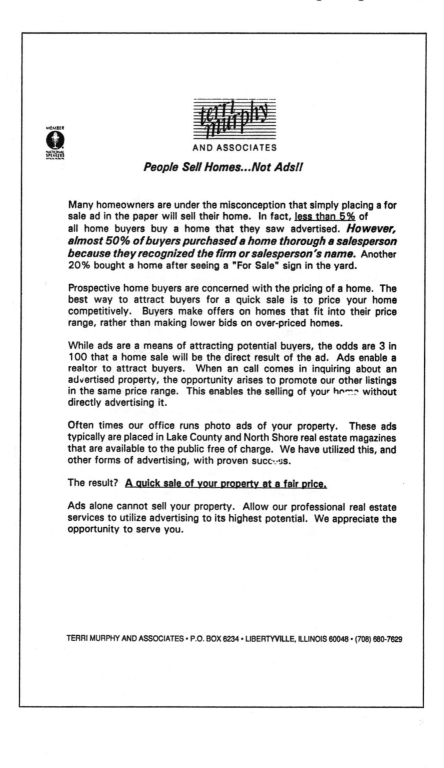

AND ASSOCIATES

People Sell Homes...Not Ads!!

Many homeowners are under the misconception that simply placing a for sale ad in the paper will sell their home. In fact, <u>less than 5%</u> of all home buyers buy a home that they saw advertised. *However, almost 50% of buyers purchased a home thorough a salesperson because they recognized the firm or salesperson's name.* Another 20% bought a home after seeing a "For Sale" sign in the yard.

Prospective home buyers are concerned with the pricing of a home. The best way to attract buyers for a quick sale is to price your home competitively. Buyers make offers on homes that fit into their price range, rather than making lower bids on over-priced homes.

While ads are a means of attracting potential buyers, the odds are 3 in 100 that a home sale will be the direct result of the ad. Ads enable a realtor to attract buyers. When an call comes in inquiring about an advertised property, the opportunity arises to promote our other listings in the same price range. This enables the selling of your home without directly advertising it.

Often times our office runs photo ads of your property. These ads typically are placed in Lake County and North Shore real estate magazines that are available to the public free of charge. We have utilized this, and other forms of advertising, with proven success.

The result? <u>A quick sale of your property at a fair price.</u>

Ads alone cannot sell your property. Allow our professional real estate services to utilize advertising to its highest potential. We appreciate the opportunity to serve you.

TERRI MURPHY AND ASSOCIATES • P.O. BOX 6234 • LIBERTYVILLE, ILLINOIS 60048 • (708) 680-7629

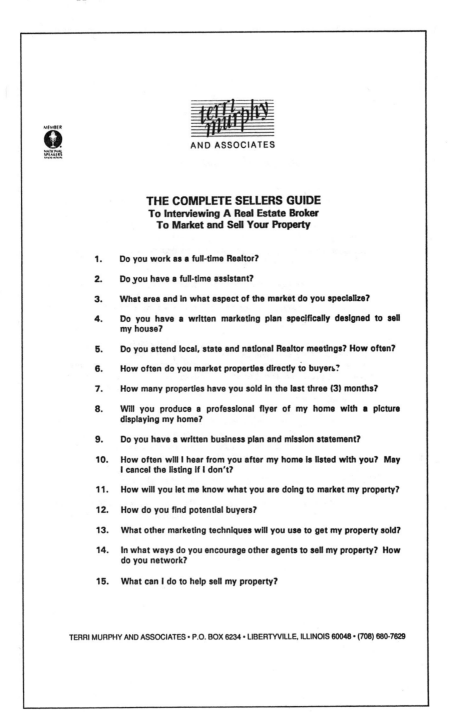

AND ASSOCIATES

THE COMPLETE SELLERS GUIDE
To Interviewing A Real Estate Broker
To Market and Sell Your Property

1. Do you work as a full-time Realtor?

2. Do you have a full-time assistant?

3. What area and in what aspect of the market do you specialize?

4. Do you have a written marketing plan specifically designed to sell my house?

5. Do you attend local, state and national Realtor meetings? How often?

6. How often do you market properties directly to buyers?

7. How many properties have you sold in the last three (3) months?

8. Will you produce a professional flyer of my home with a picture displaying my home?

9. Do you have a written business plan and mission statement?

10. How often will I hear from you after my home is listed with you? May I cancel the listing if I don't?

11. How will you let me know what you are doing to market my property?

12. How do you find potential buyers?

13. What other marketing techniques will you use to get my property sold?

14. In what ways do you encourage other agents to sell my property? How do you network?

15. What can I do to help sell my property?

TERRI MURPHY AND ASSOCIATES • P.O. BOX 6234 • LIBERTYVILLE, ILLINOIS 60048 • (708) 680-7629

TERRI MURPHY & ASSOCIATES

16.   How confident are you that you can sell my home? Why?

17.   How many listings do you have? What percentage of them sell?

18.   What is the market trend right now?

19.   Based upon what you know about my situation, should I sell?

20.   If I give you the listing, what are the first seven (7) things that you will do to sell my property in the first week?

When interviewing an agent, I believe in a level playing field. These questions are designed to tell you if the agent is taking the listing for another reason than getting your property SOLD!

* Adapted from Walter Sanford, Sanford Group Incorporated

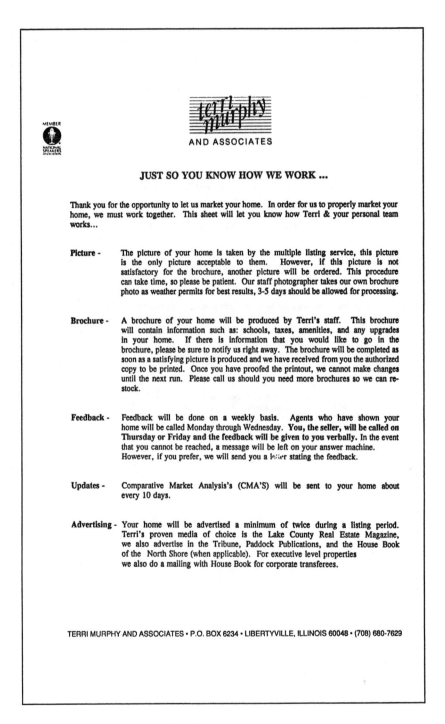

AND ASSOCIATES

JUST SO YOU KNOW HOW WE WORK ...

Thank you for the opportunity to let us market your home. In order for us to properly market your home, we must work together. This sheet will let you know how Terri & your personal team works...

Picture -   The picture of your home is taken by the multiple listing service, this picture is the only picture acceptable to them. However, if this picture is not satisfactory for the brochure, another picture will be ordered. This procedure can take time, so please be patient. Our staff photographer takes our own brochure photo as weather permits for best results, 3-5 days should be allowed for processing.

Brochure -   A brochure of your home will be produced by Terri's staff. This brochure will contain information such as: schools, taxes, amenities, and any upgrades in your home. If there is information that you would like to go in the brochure, please be sure to notify us right away. The brochure will be completed as soon as a satisfying picture is produced and we have received from you the authorized copy to be printed. Once you have proofed the printout, we cannot make changes until the next run. Please call us should you need more brochures so we can re-stock.

Feedback -   Feedback will be done on a weekly basis. Agents who have shown your home will be called Monday through Wednesday. You, the seller, will be called on Thursday or Friday and the feedback will be given to you verbally. In the event that you cannot be reached, a message will be left on your answer machine. However, if you prefer, we will send you a letter stating the feedback.

Updates -   Comparative Market Analysis's (CMA'S) will be sent to your home about every 10 days.

Advertising -   Your home will be advertised a minimum of twice during a listing period. Terri's proven media of choice is the Lake County Real Estate Magazine, we also advertise in the Tribune, Paddock Publications, and the House Book of the North Shore (when applicable). For executive level properties we also do a mailing with House Book for corporate transferees.

TERRI MURPHY AND ASSOCIATES • P.O. BOX 6234 • LIBERTYVILLE, ILLINOIS 60048 • (708) 680-7629

TERRI MURPHY & ASSOCIATES

DMS -   Direct Mail Service works with us to produce targeting marketing, list purchases, and telemarketing services.

Staging -   Terri will stage your home after we receive the listing. This includes a staging tape for you to review and Terri's own personal critiques. Also, start packing now!!! Unnecessary objects around the home can make the home look cluttered.

Utilities -   On vacant properties or before closing on your current property, utilities must be available and in working order. Agents, prospective buyers, home inspectors, and walk through's must be done with utilities on.

Showings -   Showings are for your benefit, therefore, please make every effort that your home is ready and available to show at all reasonable times. Should we decide to place a lock box on your door to make your home more accessible for showings, it will remain there until after closing so that the house is accessible for final walk through's and home inspections. We will need to keep a key in our office until the property has closed.

**Price
Changes* -**   **In the event that the market activity reflects a need to change the listing price of your home, the listing agreement date will automatically be extended for the original length of the listing period. (i.e. 90 days, 120 days)**

Offers* -   In all cases we try to present any offers in Terri's office with both brokers present. Terri's office provides the copies, teleconferencing, riders, and forms that may be necessary.

Inspections -   Home inspections can take up to three hours. Often the parties will accompany the inspector during that time. Because this service is paid for by the Buyer, the Buyers Agent will accompany the inspector

Ancillary -   Any services that are recommended by us are done only on an informational basis, and are offered as a convenience.

AND ASSOCIATES

MEMBER
NATIONAL SPEAKERS ASSOCIATION

Public Open Houses - It is our policy to discourage public access to our properties to those unqualified buyers and or non-serious prospects through public open houses. We have been able to list and sell over 100 properties per year without the use of this system. We are much more comfortable knowing the motivation and purchase power of a prospective buyer prior to exposing your home, family and personal belongings to complete strangers. If you, the seller are still in favor of public access, we will discuss those options at that time.

Our staff includes Susan Riley as Listing and Closing Coordinator and Pat Kaad as Projects and Communications Coordinator. If you have any questions about the listing process, open house, or any questions in general, please contact Susan Riley. Pat will be in touch every week, **Thursday or Friday**, with feedback from your showing. Our team is here to assist you and make your real estate transaction easier.

As an additional service, we are pleased to carry information to your attorney. However, we are not responsible for these items.

We are here to provide the finest service available. Please let us share your ideas, if we can be of further service! Thank you!!!

Acknowledge_____   _____

Date   _____

TERRI MURPHY AND ASSOCIATES • P.O. BOX 6234 • LIBERTYVILLE, ILLINOIS 60048 • (708) 680-7629

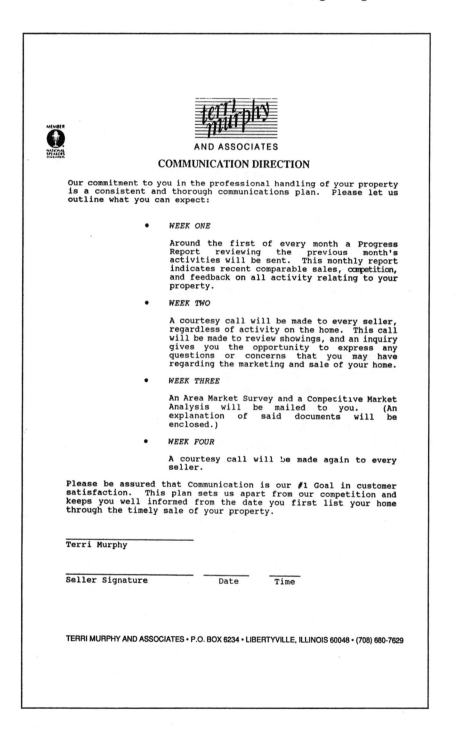

AND ASSOCIATES

COMMUNICATION DIRECTION

Our commitment to you in the professional handling of your property is a consistent and thorough communications plan. Please let us outline what you can expect:

- *WEEK ONE*

  Around the first of every month a Progress Report reviewing the previous month's activities will be sent. This monthly report indicates recent comparable sales, competition, and feedback on all activity relating to your property.

- *WEEK TWO*

  A courtesy call will be made to every seller, regardless of activity on the home. This call will be made to review showings, and an inquiry gives you the opportunity to express any questions or concerns that you may have regarding the marketing and sale of your home.

- *WEEK THREE*

  An Area Market Survey and a Competitive Market Analysis will be mailed to you. (An explanation of said documents will be enclosed.)

- *WEEK FOUR*

  A courtesy call will be made again to every seller.

Please be assured that Communication is our #1 Goal in customer satisfaction. This plan sets us apart from our competition and keeps you well informed from the date you first list your home through the timely sale of your property.

_____
Terri Murphy

_____   _____   _____
Seller Signature   Date   Time

TERRI MURPHY AND ASSOCIATES • P.O. BOX 6234 • LIBERTYVILLE, ILLINOIS 60048 • (708) 680-7629

MEMBER

NATIONAL SPEAKERS ASSOCIATION

terri murphy

AND ASSOCIATES

SELLERS HOMEWORK

Please supply original or copies of the following:

Old title policy

Survey

Mortgage paperwork

Latest tax bill

Declarations/Covenants (if applicable)

Average utilities

Information on specific assessments (if applicable)

Property information list

Copy of Personal Holiday/Christmas Mailing List

Two Keys for Front Door and Deadbolt

Signed "Just So You Know How We Work" Explanation

Homeowners/Association information

     Amount _____   Company _____

     Address _____   Contact _____

E-Mail Address

Staging/Showing Suggestions   Date _____

Interior: Basement:

Exterior: Landscaping:

Garage: Other:

Signature _____ Date _____

TERRI MURPHY AND ASSOCIATES • P.O. BOX 6234 • LIBERTYVILLE, ILLINOIS 60048 • (708) 680-7629

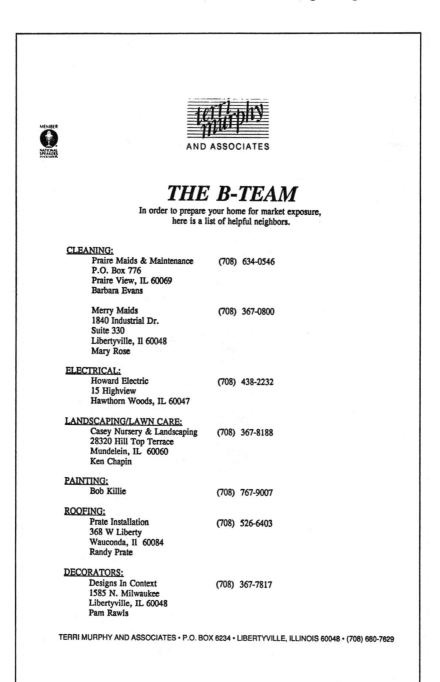

AND ASSOCIATES

THE B-TEAM

In order to prepare your home for market exposure,
here is a list of helpful neighbors.

CLEANING:
  Praire Maids & Maintenance   (708) 634-0546
  P.O. Box 776
  Praire View, IL 60069
  Barbara Evans

  Merry Maids   (708) 367-0800
  1840 Industrial Dr.
  Suite 330
  Libertyville, Il 60048
  Mary Rose

ELECTRICAL:
  Howard Electric   (708) 438-2232
  15 Highview
  Hawthorn Woods, IL 60047

LANDSCAPING/LAWN CARE:
  Casey Nursery & Landscaping   (708) 367-8188
  28320 Hill Top Terrace
  Mundelein, IL 60060
  Ken Chapin

PAINTING:
  Bob Killie   (708) 767-9007

ROOFING:
  Prate Installation   (708) 526-6403
  368 W Liberty
  Wauconda, Il 60084
  Randy Prate

DECORATORS:
  Designs In Context   (708) 367-7817
  1585 N. Milwaukee
  Libertyville, IL 60048
  Pam Rawls

TERRI MURPHY AND ASSOCIATES • P.O. BOX 6234 • LIBERTYVILLE, ILLINOIS 60048 • (708) 680-7629

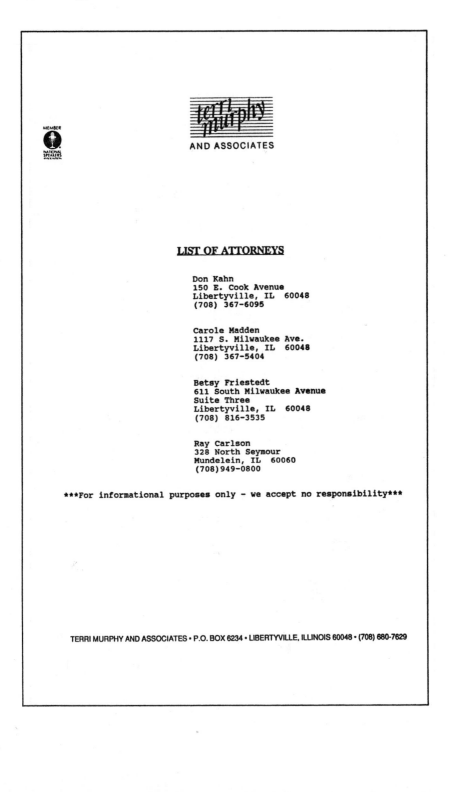

AND ASSOCIATES

MEMBER

NATIONAL
SPEAKERS
ASSOCIATION

LIST OF ATTORNEYS

Don Kahn
150 E. Cook Avenue
Libertyville, IL 60048
(708) 367-6095

Carole Madden
1117 S. Milwaukee Ave.
Libertyville, IL 60048
(708) 367-5404

Betsy Friestedt
611 South Milwaukee Avenue
Suite Three
Libertyville, IL 60048
(708) 816-3535

Ray Carlson
328 North Seymour
Mundelein, IL 60060
(708)949-0800

For informational purposes only - we accept no responsibility

TERRI MURPHY AND ASSOCIATES • P.O. BOX 6234 • LIBERTYVILLE, ILLINOIS 60048 • (708) 680-7629

Appendix B

Resource List

As a Man Thinketh, by James Allen

The Seven Habits of Highly Effective People, by Stephen Covey

First Things First, by Stephen Covey

Think & Grow Rich, by Napoleon Hill

Being Happy, by Andrew Matthews

You 2, by Price Pritchett

The Quantum Leap Strategy, by Price Pritchett

New Work Habits for a Radically Changing World, by Price Pritchett

The Stress of Organizational Change, by Price Pritchett

Mission Success, by Og Mandino (all books by Mandino are a must!)

The Prophet, by Kahlil Gibran

Unlimited Power, by Anthony Robbins

Awaken the Giant Within, by Anthony Robbins

The Man Who Would Not Be Defeated, by W. Mitchell

When God Says No, by Dr. Judith Briles

One Minute for Myself, by Spencer Johnson, M.D.

The Seven Spiritual Laws of Success, by Deepak Chopra

Ageless Body, Timeless Mind, by Deepak Chopra

Creating Affluence, by Deepak Chopra

Women Are from Venus, Men Are from Mars, by John Gray

Live Your Dreams, by Les Brown

Leadership When the Heat's On, by Danny Cox

Uncommon Friends, by James Newton

A Course in Miracles, by James Newton

Living a Beautiful Life, by Alexandra Stoddard

How To Win Customers and Keep Them for Life, by Michael LeBoeuf, PhD

Beyond Visualization, by Viki King

How To Write a Movie in 21 Days (The Inner Movie Method), by Viki King

The Magic of Thinking Big, by David J. Schwartz, PhD

How To Work a Trade Show, by Steve Miller

Wealth Strategies, by David D'Arcangelo

Streetfighter Marketing, by Jeff Slutsky

Endless Referrals, by Bob Burg

Index

About the Author

*T*erri Murphy, veteran real estate broker, is noted for her consistent high sales production and for her communication and teaching abilities. She is an extraordinary public speaker who teaches a practical and profitable "how to" philosophy. She has kept thousands spellbound with her practical approach to the sometimes difficult subject of how to make an exceptional living in the residential real estate brokerage profession.

Her credentials underscore her commitment to continuing education, both as an educator and as a student. Terri earned her Illinois real estate broker's license in 1980 and has, since then, graduated from the REALTORS® Institute and has earned her Certified Residential Specialist™ designation as well as the coveted Leadership Graduate Degree from the Women's Council of REALTORS®.

As a nationally known speaker, Terri has excelled. She has shared the stage with Ivana Trump, Susan Powter and Anthony Robbins and has worked with industry leaders David D'Arcangelo and Dr. Fred Grosse. No stranger to television and radio, Terri has been a frequent guest on "Jenny Jones" and "Twin Cities Live," and has hosted her own show, "Murphy Live on Real Estate," on the AM dial in Chicagoland. On cable TV, viewers were treated to a Terri Murphy production, "Women in Business." Her most recent endeavor in the ever-expanding television broadcasting scene is the ambitious undertaking of cofounding a national direct broadcast satellite communication and training network designed for the real estate industry.

On the literary level, Terri has had her ideas and research findings featured in books written by the best—Bob Burg, author of the very popular book *Endless Referrals*, features Terri Murphy quotes and ideas, as does Lisa Kanarek's well-researched book, *Getting Organized*. Bernard Farmer, the author of the bestselling *Time Management and Creative Disarray*, uses a great deal of Terri's well thought out and practical materials, ideas and observations.

A member of the National and Illinois Association of REALTORS®, Terri has served as chair of the prestigious publications committee and as a director of the National Association of REALTORS®.

Her achievements in real estate sales production include the "Top Listing Associate of the Year" for a major real estate franchise organization. She is a lifetime member of the Illinois Association of REALTORS® Presidents Club, where she holds the Bronze, Silver, Gold, Platinum and Diamond Awards with over 100 homes listed and sold per year for more than 17 years.